Innovative Language Teaching Practices in Higher Education in a Post-COVID Era

Edited by
Androulla Athanasiou,
Stavroulla Hadjiconstantinou,
and Maria Christoforou

]u[

ubiquity press
London

Published by
Ubiquity Press Ltd.
6 Osborn Street, Unit 3N
London E1 6TD
www.ubiquitypress.com

Text © the authors 2024

First published 2024

Cover design by Britta Zwarg
Cover image: [M] Britta Zwarg [F] phototechno / iStock /
Getty Images Plus

Print and digital versions typeset by Siliconchips Services Ltd.

ISBN (Paperback): 978-1-914481-64-2
ISBN (PDF): 978-1-914481-65-9
ISBN (EPUB): 978-1-914481-66-6
ISBN (Mobi): 978-1-914481-67-3

DOI: https://doi.org/10.5334/bdd

This work is licensed under the Creative Commons Attribution 4.0 International License (unless stated otherwise within the content of the work). To view a copy of this license, visit https://creativecommons.org/licenses/by/4.0/ or send a letter to Creative Commons, 444 Castro Street, Suite 900, Mountain View, California, 94041, USA. This license allows for copying any part of the work for personal and commercial use, providing author attribution is clearly stated.

The full text of this book has been peer-reviewed to ensure high academic standards. For full review policies, see https://www.ubiquitypress.com/

Suggested citation:
Athanasiou, A., Hadjiconstantinou, S. and Christoforou, M. (Eds.) 2024. *Innovative Language Teaching Practices in Higher Education in a Post-COVID Era*. London: Ubiquity Press. DOI: https://doi.org/10.5334/bdd. License: CC BY 4.0

To read the free, open access version of this book online, visit https://doi.org/10.5334/bdd or scan this QR code with your mobile device:

Contents

Introduction   1
*Androulla Athanasiou, Stavroulla Hadjiconstantinou,
and Maria Christoforou*

1. Rethinking CALL Teacher Education after COVID-19:
a Digital Literacies Approach   9
Cíntia Regina Lacerda Rabello

2. The role of autonomous ESP learning in acquiring
transversal professional development skills
in Higher Education   27
*Androulla Athanasiou, Elis Kakoulli Constantinou,
and Jack Burston*

3. Multimodal Reflective Journals and Life Writing:
A Didactic Approach to Enhanced Learning   49
Dana Di Pardo Léon-Henri

4. Online Practices for Teaching English Grammar
in Higher Education: Combining the flipped classroom
with digital learning paths   73
Eirini Busack

5. Integrating Critical Discourse Analysis in the Language
Classroom: A Proposed Framework for Developing
Media Critical Literacy   97
Dia Evagorou-Vassiliou

6. Turning Tables: Redesigning Virtual Exchange through the Learners' Experience   123
Laura Rampazzo, and Viviane Klen-Alves Moore

Contributors   151

Index   157

Introduction

Androulla Athanasiou,
Stavroulla Hadjiconstantinou,
and Maria Christoforou

Cyprus University of Technology, Cyprus

The landscape of Higher Education (HE) has always been dynamic, but the past few years have seen an acceleration of change that few could have predicted. The COVID-19 pandemic triggered a profound change in educational methods, forcing institutions globally to swiftly move from traditional face-to-face teaching to online and hybrid formats. This unprecedented shift not only highlighted the resilience and adaptability of educators but also exposed significant challenges and opportunities in language teaching.

How to cite this book chapter:
Athanasiou, A., Hadjiconstantinou, S. and Christoforou, M. 2024. Introduction. In: Athanasiou, A., Hadjiconstantinou, S. and Christoforou, M. (Eds.) *Innovative Language Teaching Practices in Higher Education in a Post-COVID Era*. Pp. 1–7. London: Ubiquity Press. DOI: https://doi.org/10.5334/bdd.a. License: CC BY 4.0

"Innovative Language Teaching Practices in Higher Education in a Post-COVID Era" is a timely and essential exploration of how language educators have navigated these transformative times. The contributors to this volume delve into the profound impacts of the pandemic, technological advancements, and socio-economic changes on language teaching. Through empirical research, case studies and practical suggestions they provide insights into how innovative practices are shaping the future of language education.

As we emerge from the pandemic, the question of how to effectively blend pre- and post-COVID teaching practices becomes increasingly pertinent. The research presented in this book examines the integration of traditional pedagogical methods with current digital tools and new educational paradigms. This synthesis is crucial not only for addressing the learning gaps created during the pandemic but also for preparing learners for the demands of a rapidly evolving world.

The importance of HE in this era cannot be overstated. Language instructors, in particular, are tasked with not only teaching linguistic skills but also preparing students to navigate and contribute to a complex and interconnected world. The innovative practices highlighted in this book offer valuable strategies for achieving these goals, starting with a chapter on language teacher education. In her chapter, "Rethinking CALL Teacher Education after COVID-19: a Digital Literacies Approach", Cintia Regina Lacerda Rabello explores the critical role of digital technologies in language teacher education (CTE) in Brazil, particularly heightened during the COVID-19 pandemic's Emergency Remote Teaching (ERT). It highlights the significant challenges faced by educators unprepared for integrating Computer-Assisted Language Learning (CALL) due to inadequate infrastructure and digital literacies. Studies from a Rio de Janeiro university underscore the necessity for rethinking CTE, advocating for a digital literacies approach to better equip pre-service teachers. The first study reveals how an elective course on digital literacies empowered teachers during ERT, fostering confidence in using diverse digital resources. Participants noted its relevance amidst digital divide issues exacerbated by the pandemic. The second study examines students' perspectives on ERT, emphasizing widespread digital exclusion and the inadequate integration of technologies by professors. Despite challenges, students recognized the potential of digital technologies for enhancing language learning. Both studies underscore the urgent need for comprehensive CTE reform that integrates digital technologies and literacies systematically. They advocate for a curriculum that not only equips teachers with technical skills but also fosters critical integration of technologies into pedagogical practices. The findings stress the necessity for policy changes to address digital inequality and enhance educational outcomes through innovative CTE practices aligned with contemporary digital realities.

Another important role HE is called upon to play, is the preparation of graduates in becoming employable in an ever-changing world. The demands of a competitive labor market, as highlighted by UNESCO (2015), emphasize the development of transversal skills, which education systems must now prioritize. HE institutions are thus tasked with shifting from purely academic "cognitive" skills to include essential "non-academic" skills and competencies to prepare graduates to face the challenges they will encounter in their future professions. In their chapter 'The role of autonomous ESP learning in acquiring transversal professional development skills in Higher Education', Androulla Athanasiou,

Elis Kakoulli Constantinou and Jack Burston advocate for a blended teaching approach in English for Specific Purposes (ESP) courses, leveraging cloud technologies like Google Workspace for Education to foster these skills. Project-Based Language Learning (PBLL) is proposed as an effective method to enhance learner autonomy and the development of transversal competencies. The paper provides suggestions on using various Google tools to facilitate collaborative, interactive, and flexible learning environments in ESP contexts. By integrating these technologies in the suggested PBLL approach, HE language instructors can better equip students with the necessary skills to succeed professionally and personally in a dynamic world.

Acknowledging the importance of enhancing metacognitive skills, soft skills, and self-regulation, all essential for navigating the evolving job market and personal challenges, Dana Di Pardo Léon-Henri's chapter "Multimodal Reflective Journals and Life Writing: A Didactic Approach to Enhanced Learning" underscores the transformative role of reflective journaling and life writing in tertiary education, particularly in the context of the Covid-19 pandemic and ongoing technological advancements. According to the author, reflective journaling and life writing allow students to explore personal narratives, fostering language proficiency, communication skills, empathy, and intercultural understanding. The study highlights their pedagogical value, showing how these practices promote holistic student growth and prepare graduates for diverse professional environments. Through qualitative inquiry and educational theory, the research demonstrates that engaging in reflective practices helps students develop critical self-awareness and adaptability, key competencies in a rapidly changing world.

The flipped classroom teaching method is another pedagogical model that the book explores. The chapter titled "Online Practices for Teaching English Grammar in Higher Education: Combining the Flipped Classroom with Digital Learning Paths" by Eirini Busack investigates the efficacy of integrating Digital Learning Paths (DLPs) with the flipped classroom approach to enhance grammar instruction for pre-service English teachers. This study, conducted during the COVID-19 pandemic, aims to address the sudden shift to online education by offering a seminar titled "Development of media-didactic competencies: Learning Paths & Digital Storytelling for Teaching English Grammar." The seminar employed a mixed-methods research design, including a pre- and post-seminar grammar test and an online course evaluation survey, to measure improvements in grammar knowledge and communication skills. The study revealed positive results since the participants improved their grammar knowledge, exhibiting benefits and highlighting the effective integration of technology and pedagogy. The chapter underscores the importance of combining synchronous webinars with asynchronous DLPs to foster interactive and reflective learning environments, particularly beneficial for students who are shy or reluctant to participate in traditional face-to-face settings. The study concludes that while digital media alone does not guarantee improved learning outcomes, its didactic embedding and the change in pedagogical strategies are crucial. Future research is suggested to explore further pedagogical approaches to enhance the teaching of English grammar in the post-COVID era.

Another timely theme in this volume is the role of language as a vehicle for ideology and information in an increasingly connected and digital world. The contributor explores how language educators can help students develop critical awareness of the ways in which language shapes and is shaped by societal forces. This critical perspective is essential for fostering informed and engaged global citizens. In her chapter "Integrating Critical Discourse Analysis in the Language Classroom: A Proposed Framework for Developing Media Critical Literacy, Evagorou-Vassiliou discusses the profound impact of the COVID-19 pandemic on global digital systems and media literacy, emphasizing the rise of misinformation and its detrimental effects on public trust and democratic processes. The article advocates for enhanced critical language awareness (CLA) and media literacy education, particularly in navigating the complexities of digital communication. The proposed framework integrates Critical Discourse Analysis (CDA) and Systemic Functional Grammar (SFG) to empower students with analytical tools to deconstruct media texts, identify ideological biases, and discern socio-political implications. Emphasizing a hybrid learning model that combines technology with critical pedagogy, the framework suggests practical classroom implementations such as collaborative online learning activities and guided CDA analyses of authentic media texts. By focusing on transitivity and appraisal analysis, students learn to critically assess how language constructs power dynamics, assigns responsibility, and shapes public perception. The article underscores the role of language centers in promoting critical thinking and media literacy skills, positioning educators as facilitators in preparing students to engage critically with media content. Overall, the study argues that integrating CLA and media literacy into educational curricula is essential for equipping individuals with the skills necessary to navigate and contribute responsibly to today's media-driven world.

In the book, readers can also read about Virtual Exchange (VE) as a high-impact, meaningful teaching and learning practice with the broad reach of digital technologies in a post-pandemic world. VE projects connect learners from different backgrounds and foster intercultural awareness. In their chapter "Turning Tables: Redesigning Virtual Exchange through the Learners' Experience", Laura Rampazzo and Viviane Klen-Alves Moore explore the impact of VE on Brazilian undergraduate students' language learning and intercultural competence. Using a mixed-method approach to gather both qualitative and quantitative data through structured questionnaires, their results indicate that VE effectively fosters language and intercultural learning, autonomy, and reflective practices. The participants provided insights into the program's strengths and areas for improvement and highlighted the importance of timely mediation sessions and optimized scheduling to enhance engagement. The chapter presents a learner-centered approach to VE, suggesting that integrating participants' evaluations can significantly enhance the program's effectiveness and provide valuable insights for broader application in intercultural education contexts. The analysis aligns with the teletandem framework, emphasizing social interaction, collaboration, and autonomous learning. The chapter also underscores the necessity of incorporating participants' feedback into VE redesign to better meet learners' needs and expectations.

We are confident that the insights and research presented in "Innovative Language Teaching Practices in Higher Education in a Post-COVID Era" will inspire educators, researchers, and policymakers alike. This volume is a testament to the ingenuity and dedication of language educators who continue to push the boundaries of what is possible in the pursuit of excellence in education.

Rethinking CALL Teacher Education after COVID-19: a Digital Literacies Approach

Cíntia Regina Lacerda Rabello
Universidade Federal Fluminense, Brazil
cintiarabello@id.uff.br

Abstract

CALL teacher education has long been a concern in Applied Linguistics, yet it remains neglected among many language teacher educators and institutions. Despite the ubiquity of digital technologies, they are often avoided or forbidden in Brazilian education, where laws prohibit mobile phones in classrooms. The COVID-19 pandemic forced teachers to integrate various technologies into their teaching practices during lockdowns and to continue using them for blended

How to cite this book chapter:
Rabello, C. R. L. 2024. Rethinking CALL Teacher Education after COVID-19: a Digital Literacies Approach. In: Athanasiou, A., Hadjiconstantinou, S. and Christoforou, M. (Eds.) *Innovative Language Teaching Practices in Higher Education in a Post-COVID Era.* Pp. 9–26. London: Ubiquity Press. DOI: https://doi.org/10.5334/bdd.b. License: CC BY 4.0

learning afterward. This chapter highlights the urgent need to rethink CALL teacher education in Brazilian universities, focusing on digital literacies through research at Universidade Federal Fluminense (UFF) in Rio de Janeiro. It presents findings from an action research project on pre-service teachers' perspectives in an elective discipline aimed at developing their digital literacies. Additionally, it reports on a mixed methods study of pre-service language teachers' views on online learning during the pandemic, addressing the challenges and possibilities of CALL in 'Emergency Remote Teaching' (ERT). The studies reveal that pre-service language teachers recognize the necessity to develop digital literacies and integrate technologies into teaching, as many universities lack specific CALL disciplines. Results underscore the need for innovative CALL teacher education practices to prepare future teachers to use emerging technologies effectively in post-COVID language teaching.

Introduction

Although many official documents in Brazil corroborate the relevance of digital technologies in education, they are not fully integrated into language teaching practices either due to lack of basic infrastructure, such as equipment and internet connection, or to lack of digital literacies for their pedagogical use for learning. This problem became even more evident during COVID-19, when teachers faced the challenge of using these technologies for teaching in what has been called 'Emergency Remote Teaching' (ERT). As many teachers had not been familiar with CALL, this led to misunderstandings and stressful experiences for both teachers and learners (Cardoso, 2021; Liberalli, 2020).

Thus, this chapter discusses the need to rethink CALL Teacher Education (CTE) in Brazil based on two studies conducted at a public university in Rio de Janeiro. First, it introduces an overview of CTE and digital literacies. Then, it presents the results of two studies related to CTE, as well as pre-service language teachers' views on online language learning during the pandemic. Finally, it proposes a digital literacies approach for rethinking CET practices with the effective use of digital resources for language teaching and learning.

CALL and Digital Literacies in Language Teacher Education

Language teaching has always integrated some type of technology into its practices, having relied on different technologies for each method or approach used throughout its history (Finardi & Porcino, 2014). Kessler (2018) acknowledges the varied opportunities emergent technologies, such as social media, artificial intelligence, and virtual and augmented reality, offer to enhance and promote authentic language learning. However, he also admits that although students today expect their teachers to integrate these technologies into learning, "many language teachers are unfamiliar with the extensive body of research and practice produced by professionals in the field of computer-assisted language learning (CALL)" (Kessler, 2018: 206).

This reality was observed in a study that investigated the curriculum for undergraduate and graduate programs of language teacher education at seven public universities in Brazil (Gomes, 2019). Results showed that few courses addressed CALL or digital literacies in mandatory disciplines in their regular curriculum and some universities offered elective disciplines on the topic. However, this does not guarantee that all future language teachers will develop these literacies for critical integration of technologies into their teaching practices as they leave university.

Torsani (2016: ix) also recognizes that "the use of technology in language education is still fragmentary and peripheral" as many teachers and students often limit their digital knowledge to using technology in a passive manner rather than in critical and creative ways leading to enhancement of language learning experiences. The author argues that CALL should be integrated into second language teachers' education, having as its main goal the integration of technology into language pedagogy. Moreover, he sees the relationship between linguistics and technology as a symbiotic one, in which digital technologies may be a factor of change in the pedagogy of language teaching and learning.

Thus, the author recommends the integration of CALL into the language teacher education curriculum (CTE). For him, integration does not mean simply using technologies for teaching and learning, but something that cannot be separated from this process. In other words, technologies should not be applied to language learning as an additional element, but rather, as an integral part of the pedagogy of language teaching and learning. According to Torsani, second language teacher education should embrace CALL in its curriculum to develop teachers' CALL competencies and digital skills.

A similar view is shared by Pegrum, Hockly, and Dudeney (2022), who acknowledge the need for language teachers to understand and integrate a variety of digital literacies into the language curriculum. The authors argue that the transformations we have been facing during the past decades, such as sociopolitical changes, globalization, rise of superdiversity, physical and digital mobility, and the spread of misinformation, disinformation and fake news, in addition to challenges such as climate change, terrorism, wealth gaps and pandemics, "make it imperative to develop the kind of literacies that can facilitate collaboration across languages and worldviews in face-to-face, digital, and blended contexts" (*ibid*: 3).

Thus, the authors present a Framework of Digital Literacies 3.0 to help language teachers and educators "make sense of what digital literacies now mean, and how to operationalize them in learning designs which are appropriate to students' needs in the third decade of the 21st century" (*ibid*: 2). This framework contains four focus areas that comprise a great variety of literacies: (1) communicating, which includes print, texting, hypertext, multimodal, immersive, special, mobile, code and AI literacies; (2) informing, including tagging, search, filtering, information and data literacies; (3) collaborating, including personal, security, network, participatory, intercultural and ethical literacies; and (4) (re)designing, which includes attentional, critical and remix literacies.

In previous work, Dudeney, Hockly & Pegrum (2016) argue that for language teaching to remain meaningful, teachers must encompass varied digital literacies in their lessons and develop students' literacies. However, to do that, second language teacher education must include these literacies in language teaching and learning practices. Finally, the authors emphasize the need to incorporate activities into the language curriculum that work this wide range of literacies in the development of students' linguistic and technological competencies, as well as teachers' own technological competence and digital literacies.

Hence, language teacher education needs to rethink and redesign its curriculum to integrate digital technologies and literacies and embrace CTE. It can also be argued that one of the many difficult lessons we have learned from ERT is that both CALL and digital literacies can no longer be neglected in language teacher education curricula and practices.

Methods and Process

This chapter presents the results of two studies conducted with pre-service language teachers in Brazil investigating their perspectives on CTE and the use of digital technologies for teaching and learning before and during COVID-19. Both studies have been approved by the ethics committee at UFF. The participants signed an informed consent to participate in the study and all names were substituted by pseudonyms or numbers.

The first study comprises an action research that focused on pre-service teachers' perspectives on CTE in an elective discipline aimed at developing future teachers' digital literacies. The discipline was planned, implemented, and evaluated as part of the action research cycle (Tripp, 2005) and consistently redesigned from 2017 to 2021, according to participants' and researcher's evaluation. For this chapter, a micro study conducted in April 2020 is presented. This study was carried out at the beginning of the pandemic with students who had participated in the discipline from 2017 to 2019. The qualitative study investigated the contributions of the elective discipline to their practice as language teachers during ERT. Online interviews conducted by e-mail (Mann & Stewart, 2002) aimed at identifying whether and how the elective discipline had helped them develop the necessary digital literacies to navigate language teaching in ERT and the challenges and opportunities they were facing at that moment when they had to teach exclusively online.

Participants comprised six teachers who answered positively to the invitation sent by e-mail to the 26 pre-service teachers who had concluded the CALL elective discipline between 2017 and 2019. All of them were working as language teachers in private or public institutions in March 2020, when the pandemic was declared in Brazil and many schools and universities closed and classes had to be taught online for about two years.

The second study is a mixed methods study (Mann & Stewart, 2002) focused on pre-service teachers' views on online language learning at Brazilian universities during ERT. Participants comprised 40 undergraduate language students from six different universities in Brazil who studied exclusively online between 2020 and 2021 and answered the online questionnaire agreeing to participate in the study.

Research instruments comprised an online questionnaire and online interviews. The online questionnaire was designed in *Google Forms* consisting of 17 closed questions and nine open questions and shared on *Facebook* Communities of Language and Arts undergraduate students at Brazilian universities besides the student representatives at UFF from June to August 2022. Due to length limitations, only the results of the online questionnaire will be presented in this chapter.

The results of both studies were analysed in the light of Bardin's (2009) content analysis and the extracts taken from participants' answers to questionnaires and interviews were translated into English.

Results

The results of the first study indicate that all six teachers acknowledged the relevance of the elective discipline to their teaching practices during ERT, highlighting the repertoire of digital literacies and technologies they had learned as the biggest contribution of the course. The excerpts below show participants' perceptions of the course:

> 'Today, I am more confident to use some resources both for research on the topic that my school was responsible for preparing and for preparing the didactic sequences.' (Jéssica)

> 'The course showed a range of digital resources that can be used in education, encouraging creativity and student participation, [...] the discipline was essential to teach how to use these resources as allies in the teaching-learning process, especially at this moment when classes are being completely online.' (Laura)

> 'I feel very confident using the tools, even those that we didn't see in class, due to the basis that I acquired during the course. It gave me great relief to know how to use the tools and have a range of options to choose from and test, and I was able to share what I knew with my colleagues.' (Míriam)

Although the teaching realities of the participants were quite different in terms of available resources and institutional support, most of them mentioned the challenges of ERT as being related to the lack of internet access or connectivity problems and the scarcity of formal CTE. Many participants mentioned being able to help their colleagues, who did not have any experience with CALL, due to the opportunity of taking the elective discipline. Another important concern shared by participants was the enormous digital divide existent in Brazil and that became more evident during the pandemic as many students (and teachers) did not have access to appropriate equipment and devices and/or good internet connection to carry out their academic and professional activities.

Despite the challenges, participants were also able to perceive some opportunities related to ERT, such as the possibility to use different digital resources in online classes, which was not possible before as some institutions lacked infrastructure and technologies for language classes, and also the lessons learned from this period, showing the relevance of CTE, as illustrated in the extract below:

> 'When there are no connection issues (interrupted connection, audio dropping out, etc.), which unfortunately happens frequently, the classes have been interesting and fruitful.' (Laura)

The quote highlights the necessity of investments in basic technology infrastructure and digital literacies as a national public policy. Moreover, CALL teacher education is also urgent to enable language teachers to make effective use of digital technologies for teaching and learning in different scenarios and situations that go beyond pandemic times. These results reinforce the need to rethink CALL as part of the language teacher education curriculum in Brazil, which should include digital literacies as a core element in pre-service teacher education.

The second study was conducted in the post-COVID period and investigated the impacts of ERT from the perspective of pre-service language teachers. As digital exclusion was a topic of great concern during the pandemic, two questions in the online questionnaire aimed at identifying the main devices and type of internet connection used by students during ERT. Figure 1 shows the devices students used for ERT and, for this question, participants could indicate more than one option. According to the graphic, it can be inferred that, although many students used desktop or laptop computers, mobile phones were used by most students (90%) during ERT.

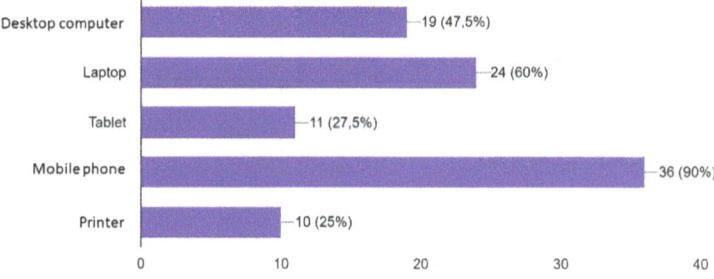

Figure 1: Devices used for online learning during ERT.
Source: The author.

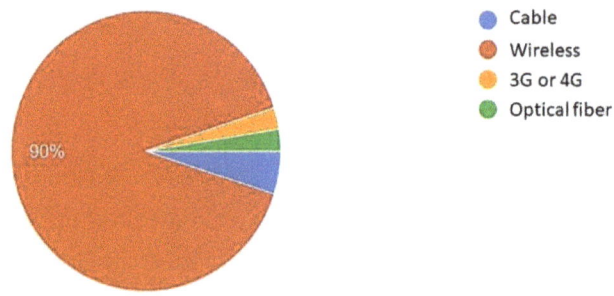

Figure 2: Type of Internet connection used during ERT.
Source: The author.

Figure 2 shows the type of connection students used for online activities during ERT and it shows that despite many problems related to bad internet connection, the most common type of internet connection used by students was wireless (90%).

Due to the concern related to massive digital exclusion, many public universities offered financial support programs to help students buy mobile phones, tablets, or SIM cards with internet connection. However, only 10% of students declared having received help to acquire digital devices to be able to participate in online classes during ERT. Also, few students reported having had difficulties in using the digital platforms and/or technologies used by their professors and institutions (37,5%).

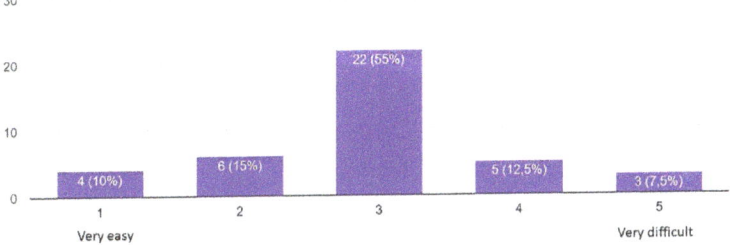

Figure 3: Participants' assessment of their learning during ERT.
Source: The author.

Participants were also asked to assess their learning experience during ERT using a Likert Scale of 5 points, being 1 very easy and 5 very difficult. As shown in Figure 3, most students (55%) considered their learning experience during ERT period as not very easy or very difficult.

Participants were also asked to indicate the main difficulties they faced during ERT. The content analysis of the open answers identified the main difficulties being related to: (1) lack of (adequate) equipment; (2) lack of quality internet connection; (3) initial difficulty in adapting to new online platforms; (4) fatigue due to long exposure to screens; (5) lack of appropriate environment for remote classes, which sometimes prevented them from using their cameras and/or microphones; and (6) lack of professors' preparation for online lessons and poor organization of materials in the Virtual Learning Environments (VLEs). Some of the answers that illustrate these difficulties are presented below:

> 'In remote teaching, we have many variants. Devices that are not very good, laptop that crashes during class. Internet that crashes or slows down, lack of an environment conducive to studying. Unfortunately for me it hasn't worked.' (P7)

> 'I was not familiar with some platforms; I didn't know how to use them and so I had difficulty doing some activities or simply stopped doing them.' (P18)
>
> 'I shared a tablet and computer with my sister during ERT. This made reading very difficult. One always had to give the device to another. In addition, there were issues with the internet and I missed some assessment activities because of that.' (P17)
>
> '[...] many professors are not prepared to teach online, we are not only under the pressure of learning the subject at college, but also having to learn how to manage our time between work and study... [...] Some professors didn't know how to organize Moodle very well, so it was difficult to find/post activities and texts. [...]' (P4)
>
> 'Tiring period, a lot of time with the screen exposed in front of your eyes.' (P19)

Besides these difficulties, participants claimed their greatest difficulty during ERT as being related to: (1) internet connection problems; (2) lack of student participation, interaction and work with orality in online lessons; (3) exhaustion; (4) the lesson models used by some professors, which consisted of transposition of face-to-face classes to the online environment; (5) lack of concentration; (6) no clear separation between the family environment and the work/study environment; (7) lack of discipline; (8) excessive number of reading tasks; and (9) physical separation from professors and classmates.

Moreover, 32 students considered ERT as harming their physical or mental health, mentioning the following problems: (1) anxiety, low self-esteem, and depression; (2) backaches and vision problems; (3) headaches and mental exhaustion; (4) obesity; (5) burnout; and (6) insomnia. On the other hand, seven students reported feeling no negative impact. As justifications for their answers, they mentioned ERT helped them keep their minds busy during lockdown and one of them mentioned having faced anxiety problems when returning to face-to-face classes at university.

Besides the problems aforementioned, most students (28) could also perceive positive impacts on language learning mediated by digital technologies citing as its main contributions: (1) greater contact with digital technologies and platforms; (2) greater range of features; (3) development of autonomy and independence; (4) possibility of rewatching recorded classes; and (5) possibility of interaction with native speakers via CMC. Only six students did not perceive any positive impact on their learning, mentioning online lessons as nonproductive and associating it with a mechanization of the teaching activity.

Finally, the last question in the questionnaire aimed at identifying whether students would like to continue using technologies for language learning after the pandemic, making use of CALL in their pre-service teacher education. Most students (70%) stated they would like to continue using digital technologies for language learning in face-to-face classes after the pandemic, 20% were not sure, choosing the option "maybe" and only one student (2,5%) reported not wanting to use digital technologies for language learning after COVID-19, probably due to negative experiences. Some of the technologies students mentioned wanting to continue using are illustrated in the extracts below:

> 'I would like to maintain the use of technologies for consulting materials and for communicating with colleagues and teachers, in addition to feeling less pressured with the online assessment system, which allows for greater flexibility and more time to articulate ideas.' (P1)

> 'I would like to be able to continue using all the technologies used so far (and perhaps new ones) to carry

out research, assignments, presentations, compositions, tests, and various assessments, both written and oral.' (P6)

Although the questionnaire did not approach the development of digital literacies during ERT, it is possible to identify different literacies that were developed in that period in the extracts above, such as those related to communicating, informing, and collaborating as described by Pegrum; Hockly & Dudeney 2022. Additionally, many pre-service teachers acknowledged the relevance of technology integration to language teaching and learning.

Furthermore, the results of the second study revealed that most students and many professors were not familiar with CALL before the pandemic and were 'forced' to use digital technologies to continue their courses, leading to negative impacts not only to their learning experiences but also to their mental and physical health. Besides problems related to digital exclusion and appropriate infrastructure for ERT, the negative impacts may be related to the fact that these technologies were not used properly in a way to promote greater interaction among learners, professors, and content and enhance language learning as it is the aim of CALL practices.

Discussion

Despite having different objectives, both studies present pre-service language teachers' perspectives on the use of digital technologies for teaching and learning languages and their teacher education. The first study shows how the elective discipline has helped them face the need to teach online using technologies during ERT. Participants perceived the contributions and relevance of the discipline for their teacher education and the applicability of what they had learned in the context of COVID-19. Concurrently, it is important to note that, as there is no mandatory discipline in the language teaching curriculum at the investigated institution, very few students enrolled in the elective discipline from 2017 to 2019, being prepared to teach and learn effectively with the use of digital technologies when COVID-19 started.

The second study shows language students' perspectives and experiences on ERT, evidencing the lack of CALL teacher education, as many professors had problems integrating technologies into their teaching, leading to negative impacts on students' learning and also physical and mental health. As many professors had no teacher education on CALL or online learning, many ERT experiences involved a transposition of face-to-face lessons to virtual platforms with most classes consisting of synchronous activities conducted on platforms such as *Google Meet* and *Zoom*, which may have impacted future language teachers negatively concerning CALL and online learning (Cardoso, 2021;Liberalli 2020). On the other hand, they were also able to identify positive impacts of ERT on their learning and future language teaching practices, such as using different technologies and how not to teach online.

Thus, the results of both studies evidence the need for innovative CALL teacher education practices so that future teachers can develop their digital literacies and integrate emergent technologies into future language teaching practices in meaningful and effective ways in the post-COVID era. Hence, a digital literacy approach, as suggested by Pegrum, Hockly & Dudeney (2022) can benefit preservice language teachers as the development of these literacies is paramount for social practices in contemporary society.

Conclusion

As many Brazilian universities still do not have a specific discipline on CALL or technology-enhanced language learning in their curricula (Gomes, 2019), it is suggested that teachers and curriculum designers learn from the ERT experience during COVID-19 and adopt and integrate digital technologies not only to teaching and learning practices but also to the teacher education curriculum, rethinking CALL teacher education to promote innovative CALL practices through a digital literacies approach, developing future teachers' digital literacies throughout their course as suggested by Torsani (2016), Pegrum, Hockly & Dudeney (2022) and Gomes (2019).

As mobile phones were cited as an important technology for learning practices during COVID-19, we may also consider MALL (Mobile-Assisted Language Learning) practices in preservice language teacher education (Kukulska-Hulme, 2018) as these devices have pervaded most of our social practices and are an inextricable part of our students' lives. As language educators, we need to rethink the use of these devices in our language lessons so that students can develop their mobile literacy (Pegrum, Hockly & Dudeney, 2022) and take advantage of these technologies for language learning, being able to incorporate B.Y.O.D. (Bring Your Own Device) practices, for example.

Furthermore, future language teachers acknowledge the relevance of digital technologies for teaching and learning practices and the urgent need to develop their digital literacies. This could be noticed in the fact that many language professors and students had not been familiarized with these technologies before COVID-19, misusing them in their practices and leading to both physical and mental issues during ERT.

Finally, the results of both studies evidence the great digital inequality and exclusion that is still alarming in Brazil and that was highlighted and even increased during COVID-19. This resulted in many students failing or quitting their studies due to lack of access to digital devices, internet connection, and even digital literacies. Thus, besides the need for innovative CTE practices, we need public policies in Brazil that not only promote both access to devices and good internet connection to all citizens but also ensure the development of digital literacies throughout their education.

References

Bardin, L. (2009). Análise de Conteúdo. Lisboa: Edições 70.

Cardoso, J. (2021). Formação crítico-reflexiva de professores de línguas em tempos de
crise: implementando o "inédito viável" em "situações-limite". In J. Cardoso & P. Arantes (Orgs.), Diálogos sobre ensino e aprendizagem em tempos de resistência. Rio de Janeiro: Cartolina, 2021 (pp. 14–25).

Dudeney, G., Hockly, N. & Pegrum, M. (2016). Letramentos Digitais. Translated by Marcos Marcionilo. 1st ed. São Paulo: Parábola Editorial.

Finardi, K. R. & Porcino, M. C. (2014). Tecnologia e metodologia no ensino de inglês: impactos da globalização e da internacionalização. Ilha Desterro, 66, 239–283.

Gomes, F. W. B. (2019). Letramento Digital e Formação de Professores nos Cursos de Letras de Universidades Federais Brasileiras. Teresina: EDUFPI.

Kessler, G. (2018). Technology and the future of language teaching. Foreign language Annuals, 51(1), 205–218.

Kukulska-Hulme, A. (2018). Mobile-assisted language learning [Revised and updated version]. In: C. A. Chapelle (Ed.) The Concise Encyclopedia of Applied Linguistics. Wiley. Retrieved from: https://oro.open.ac.uk/57023/ in May 2024.

Liberalli, F. (2020). Construir o inédito viável em meio a crise do coronavírus – lições que aprendemos, vivemos e propomos. In F. Liberalli et al. (Orgs.) Educação em tempos de pandemia: brincando com um mundo possível. Campinas: Pontes, 2020 (pp. 13–21).

Mann, C. & Stewart, F. (2002). Internet Communication and qualitative research: a handbook for researching online. London: SAGE Publications.

Pegrum, M., Hockly, N. & Dudeney, G. (2022). Digital Literacies. 2nd Edition. New York: Routledge. DOI: https://doi.org/10.4324/9781003262541

Torsani, S. (2016). CALL Teacher Education: language teachers and technology integration. Rotterdam: Sense Publishers.

Tripp, D. (2005) Pesquisa-ação: uma introdução metodológica. Educação e Pesquisa, *31*(3), 443–466.

The role of autonomous ESP learning in acquiring transversal professional development skills in Higher Education

Androulla Athanasiou, Elis Kakoulli Constantinou, and Jack Burston
Cyprus University of Technology, Cyprus
androulla.athanasiou@cut.ac.cy, elis.constantinou@cut.ac.cy, and jack.burston@cut.ac.cy

Abstract

The rapid developments in a globalised 21st Century world have brought about changes and increased competitiveness in the employability of graduates. Acknowledging these developments and the need for innovation, the European Union recognises the need for education and training beyond

---

How to cite this book chapter:
Athanasiou, A., Kakoulli Constantinou, E. and Burston, J. 2024. The role of autonomous ESP learning in acquiring transversal professional development skills in Higher Education. In: Athanasiou, A., Hadjiconstantinou, S. and Christoforou, M. (Eds.) *Innovative Language Teaching Practices in Higher Education in a Post-COVID Era*. Pp. 27–48. London: Ubiquity Press. DOI: https://doi.org/10.5334/bdd.c. License: CC BY 4.0

the classroom (UNESCO, 2020). Hence, Higher Education (HE) is crucial in developing transversal skills and preparing undergraduates for the labour market. Essential therefore is developing independent learning habits and a collaborative lifelong learning mindset. Likewise, competence in English at a B1 CEFR (Common European Framework of References for Languages) level is a prerequisite of independent learning in any field. Lastly, autonomous learning also depends on knowing how to exploit ubiquitous digital technologies to extend language learning into daily life. This paper aims to provide suggestions to practitioners about how the teaching of English for Specific Purposes (ESP) courses need to be approached as a critical autonomous learning skill for professional knowledge acquisition, task accomplishment and interpersonal communication. It advocates for a blended teaching and learning mode, tailored to future graduates' needs. Cloud technologies, such as Google Workspace for Education (Google, 2023), potentially offer an effective type of support for the development of transversal competencies in the context of ESP in HE.

Introduction

In recent years, the role of education has moved increasingly in the direction of preparing graduates to become employable in an ever rapidly changing world. In particular, owing to the demands of a competitive labour market as reflected in reports published by UNESCO (2015) with regards to the development of transversal skills, education is called upon to prepare future citizens to meet the requirements of employers. Therefore, there is much discussion worldwide, with regards to what quality education and learning in the 21st century entails (European Commission, 2017). In these discussions, what is highlighted is the urgent need for educational systems and Higher Education, in particular to shift from the pure accumulation of academic "cognitive" skills to hard-to-measure "non-academic" skills and competencies. The amassing of these skills and competencies (e.g., efficient communication, innovative thinking, teamwork, problem solving, etc.) not only helps students become adequately prepared for the labour market but is also essential in ensuring that future generations are equipped with transversal skills to survive and flourish in a rapidly changing world. It is especially important that these competencies be developed in order to enable students to learn autonomously and become lifelong learners.

This paper initially discusses the importance of transversal skills and how transdisciplinary knowledge can be combined with these skills in English for Specific Purposes (ESP) courses in Higher Education. The aim is to provide some practical suggestions, considering the challenges faced in language teaching and learning, as to how these ESP courses can be approached and how a blended mode of teaching and learning can be adopted in order to meet the needs of future graduates. To accomplish this objective, it is proposed that cloud technologies and Google Workspace for Education (Google, 2023) in particular, be exploited to support transversal competencies in the context of ESP in Higher Education.

Transversal Skills and Language Learning

Transversal skills (also referred to as soft skills, 21st century skills, etc.) are considered as skills that "are not specifically related to a particular job, task, academic discipline or area of knowledge and that can be used in a wide variety of situations and work settings"

(UNESCO IBE, 2013). The development of transversal skills has been the topic of considerable attention in educational discussions in recent years, reaching particular prominence in the UNESCO reports (2015, 2016). In essence, the development of transversal skills is intended to expand how learning takes place and how it is applied across academic and professional disciplines, communities and cultures, rather than just possessing the knowledge of how to perform a task, i.e. hard skills which can be measured (Mishra, 2014).

In particular, the Education Research Institutes Network (ERI-Net) working group divides transversal skills in six main categories: critical and innovative thinking, intrapersonal skills, interpersonal skills, media and information literacy, global citizenship and others (UNESCO, 2016). Under these domains are included skills, such as creative problem-solving, communication, teamwork, persuasion, negotiation and leadership among others (Majid et al., 2012) which are of vital importance in dealing with the competitiveness and challenges faced in the labour market. Moreover, the European Union (UNESCO, 2020), recognises the role of education and training in developing these competencies.

The learning of foreign (FL) and second languages (L2) plays a pivotal role in the development of transversal skills, since the teaching of languages involves the development of plurilingualism (or 'multilingualism'), as well as the skill of understanding different settings, relationships and cultural backgrounds (ECML, 2021). So, too, the teaching of FL and L2 is not confined to a particular topic, thus fostering space to pursue transversality (ibid.).

The role of and interest in transversality and transdisciplinarity in relation to the teaching of English as a second/foreign language is not new (Jaganathan et al., 2014). According to Jaganathan et al. (ibid.), English plays a critical role in disciplinary learning and intercultural communication, the very bedrock of transdisciplinarity and transversality. Given the *lingua franca* status of English in virtually all spheres of disciplinary learning, its use needs to begin early in learners' formal education. Achieving this goal requires teachers to act as guides and scaffolders. However, it is equally important that students develop a strong mindset of self-direction and autonomy.

The development of transversal skills requires a degree of learner autonomy and vice versa. According to Fleisher (2009, p. 1), 'learning is enhanced as children become in charge of their learning by being supported in autonomy as well as the development of academic competencies', including transversal skills (Centre for Responsive Schools Inc, 2018). In such a case, learners engage actively and constructively in the learning process, in which they set goals and monitor their learning, thus developing both cognitive and metacognitive skills (Bosmans et al., 2023). Learners' active involvement in the learning process is also stressed in contemporary theories of learning such as social constructivism and connectivism. For social constructivist approaches to learning, knowledge is constructed through the interaction of learners' past experiences and ideas with experiences and activities which they come in contact with (Richardson, 1997). For social constructivism people learn when they are involved in social interaction, collaboration and problem-solving activities. Connectivism has similarities with social constructivism in the sense that social interaction has a prominent role. For connectivism, learning can reside outside of ourselves; it can occur through networks (Siemens, 2005).

In order, therefore, to foster the autonomous development of transversal skills as well as learner autonomy, Project Based Language Learning (PBLL) could be a possible method to be incorporated in language education (Guven & Valais, 2014). PBLL in general is 'a particular type of inquiry-based learning where the context of learning is provided through authentic questions and problems within real-world practices that lead to meaningful learning experiences' (Kokotsaki et al., 2016, p. 267). PBLL, according to Guven & Valais (2014), 'can be used to help direct English language learners towards autonomy through well planned stages of learning that emphasise interaction, critical thinking, problem-solving and collaboration' (p.184), thus emphasising how transversal skills are developed.

Hence, once learners leave school and / or graduate from a HE institution and are on their own, they can keep up professionally through their English language skills and develop transversal competencies applied to self-directed, autonomous efforts.

ESP: transdisciplinary knowledge & development of transversal skills

By their very nature, ESP courses offer cognitive skills in the field of study of the learners in the English language, based 'on an assessment of purposes and needs and the activities for which English is needed' (Rahman, 2015, p. 24). ESP courses therefore need to smoothly blend interpersonal and academic communication skills, in order to provide opportunities for learning and practising context-specific language (Chalikandy, 2013). In these courses, learners are provided with readings (e.g., research, reports, etc.), which they may encounter as future professionals and citizens and which they will need in order to keep up to date (Graddol, 2000). To effectively access these resources, reading fluency in the language needs to be maintained at a near native level (i.e., CEFR C2). L2 learners' listening comprehension also needs to reach this level in order to understand and evaluate professionally related information. Likewise, with English being the lingua franca of international professional meetings (Barančicová & Zerzová, 2015), an advanced-low level (i.e., CEFR B2) of listening comprehension is a minimal requirement for attendees. In the case of delivering oral presentations themselves at such meetings, professionals need to have at least advanced-mid English-speaking skills (i.e., CEFR C1). More generally, with the rapid development of information technology, they need to possess at least an overall intermediate level (i.e., CEFR B1+) of English language competence. However, ESP courses in higher education do not teach English for 'specified needs' (Johnson & Johnson, 1998, p. 105) alone.

According to Jiang et al. (2022), in the past few decades, transversal skills, such as teamwork, communication and problem-solving, have become an integral part of universities' educational objectives, aiming to develop professional lifelong learning. Considering that such skills depend on the ability to understand, empathise and effectively communicate with others, not only in the workplace, but in society in general, this is where ESP courses play an important role. From a language learning perspective, engaging students in collaborative tasks provides them with the opportunity to communicate, collaborate and complete their tasks. It is through this communication that learners practise what they have learned (Sinkus, 2020). This is also true of disciplinary knowledge. Through communicative and collaborative project-based activities, students not only learn and share disciplinary information, but they also synthesise and internalise that knowledge. Collaboration requires negotiation of meaning, which is as essential for language learning as it is for critical thinking and disciplinary knowledge acquisition and to a greater extent for autonomous and lifelong learning (ibid.).

In theory, the focus on developing transversal skills in ESP courses in HE is an attempt that would be successful in ideal settings in which learners already have a developed mindset of self-direction. However, in practice, instructors are faced with a number of daily challenges, among which are student resistance (Yi-Ping, 2018), lack of student engagement (Mystkowska-Wiertelak, 2022), collaborative skills (Casper, 2017), critical thinking skills (Fadhlullah & Ahmad, 2017), as well as lack of autonomy. The parameters and the scope of the above challenges may differ according to each context in various studies. However, these are common challenges faced in language learning and teaching contexts.

In order to overcome or reduce these challenges and at the same time develop language learners' transversal skills, they could engage in Project-Based Language Learning (PBLL), as appropriate for their field of study. The key here is to make it professionally and personally relevant, interesting and authentic (Tuyen & Tien, 2021; Kokotsaki et al., 2016). Students can be divided into small groups to discover each other's interests, which can then be matched to the thematic units of the curriculum.

At a first stage, the above process should be teacher guided by instructing students about the steps they need to take (Bell, 2010). This may take some extra time for teachers to prepare, but once students have been prepared, instructors need only track their progress. Teachers can suggest websites to find information and explain why these websites are best for searching, without instructing exactly how the project should be structured. Teachers should encourage students to take initiatives and allow space for decision making as to how they will achieve their end product (Prastiwi et al., 2021; Tuyen & Tien, 2021; Rodríguez-Peñarroja, 2022).

Overall, working on something that interests them with others who share the same interests can encourage collaboration (Casper, 2017), critical thinking (Socciarelli et al., 2020), negotiation and creativity (Thuan, 2018), thus developing those transversal skills necessary for their further studies, their future profession, professional development as well as their lives. Consequently, their engagement may also increase (Aubrey, 2022), if they are allowed to be innovative, take initiatives and use technologies that will help them carry out their project.

Hence, working on projects iteratively in ESP courses can allow students to further develop their transversal skills and eventually take charge of their own learning, and thus develop learner autonomy. To this effect, the development and use of Information and Communications Technologies (ICT) could be used to contribute to the pedagogy of ESP courses and to the development of those transversal skills that will enable learners to succeed in both their academic and professional ventures.

Cloud technologies:
The case of Google Workspace for Education

The integration of ICT in education has allowed the transition of teacher-centred traditional classrooms to student-centred educational environments (Almendo, 2020) and has transferred the responsibility of the learning process to the learner. Cloud technologies or cloud computing in particular, belong to a category of ICT that can significantly enhance PBLL by providing a dynamic, interactive, and resource-rich environment, and thus facilitate the development of transversal competencies in the context of language education. Especially in ESP contexts, where educators and learners need access to information pertaining to specific disciplines, the qualities of cloud technologies could be invaluable.

To understand the value of cloud technologies for language learning in general and ESP in particular, it is useful first of all to focus on their attributes and characteristics. According to the National Institute of Standards and Technology (2021), cloud computing is "a model for enabling ubiquitous, convenient, on-demand network access to a shared pool of configurable computing resources (e.g., networks, servers, storage, applications and services) that can be rapidly provisioned and released with minimal management effort or service provider interaction". Through the years certain concerns have been expressed with regards to the use of cloud technologies in education, such as uncertainty over their cost in the future, the lack of user control over these technologies and issues of reliability, security and privacy. Nevertheless, cloud computing offers great potential benefits for educational organisations and its viability has been confirmed many times in CALL literature (Sultan, 2010; Lakshminarayanan et al., 2013; Pokrovska et al., 2020). The various attributes of cloud technologies foster synchronous and asynchronous collaboration and communication and provide access to a variety of resources and therefore facilitate the implementation of PBLL practices, creating an interactive flexible learning environment.

Google Workspace for Education is one of the most popular examples of cloud technologies for education. It is a set of tools and services provided by Google which are tailored for schools and educational institutions in general to collaborate, streamline instruction and allow for learning to occur in a safe environment (Google, 2023). The tools and services offered by Google Workspace for Education can foster social constructivist and connectivist approaches to learning. They allow for collaboration, communication, organisation of different tasks and material and maintain the connection between users, and therefore have the potential for creating an ideal environment for the implementation of PBLL and the development of transversal competencies. Additionally, they may promote students' responsibility and learner autonomy. They can individualise the learning process and enhance self-study and students can learn at their own pace having an enormous amount of materials and resources at their disposal (Borova et al., 2021).

Google tools have been used extensively in education and in language classrooms in particular. There are many examples of how they can be utilised to develop learner autonomy and create a lifelong learning mentality. Almendo (2020) describes how Google forms and Google Translate can be employed to provide support and minimise reading challenges when students are engaged in reading tasks in a language class. Drawing on the challenges that COVID-19 brought about, Dantes et al. (2022) elaborate on the use of Google classroom in a vocational school in Bali in an online context. Their study showed that despite the challenges faced, the use of Google Classroom was positively perceived by the students from cognitive, affective and behavioural perspectives. It also showed the importance of teacher's guidance in a learning journey on which students had to embark autonomously due to the situation. Furthermore, Xie et al. (2019) discuss how Google Expeditions, an interactive Virtual Reality tool can be used in an advanced Chinese language class easing cognitive burden and increasing students' interest in the target culture and their motivation.

The potential of the use of Google tools for the development of transversal competences and an autonomous and lifelong learning mindset can just as well be experienced in HE ESP contexts and this is where discussion will focus on in the next section.

Google Workspace for Education as a medium for the development of transversal competencies and learner autonomy in ESP contexts

Examples of employment of Google tools in HE language courses can be found across the globe. Susilawati (2023) discusses the positive views of students on the use of Google Docs for the development of academic writing skills at a private Indonesian university, stressing students' comments on Google Docs direct checking of their writing, the auto saving and auto translation modes, the feedback from the lecturer, their engagement in collaborative writing and the possibility to write in an organised manner. Similarly, Humeniuk et al. (2023) describe the use of Google applications for ESP teaching in Ukraine during wartime, concluding that Google applications and more specifically Google Meet and Google Classroom, are preferred by students, improving the motivational, cognitive, technological and social aspects of the educational process. On the same note, another study from Ukraine (Benadla & Hadji, 2021) reports on the positive results from the utilisation of Google tools in an ESP context at Taras Shevchenko National University of Kyiv during the COVID-19 pandemic. Examples of the employment of Google tools in ESP environments can also be found in the Cypriot Higher Education context again with satisfactory results for both students and course instructors (Kakoulli Constantinou, 2018). In all the aforementioned studies, apart from the fact that participants believe that these tools have enhanced their knowledge acquisition, it can be inferred that these tools have also facilitated the development of students' transversal competencies as well as autonomous learning skills.

The flexibility of Google Workspace for Education tools creates an ideal environment for the implementation of PBLL and the cultivation of transversal competencies. Table 1 shows some examples of how Google Workspace for Education can accommodate PBLL practices.

Steps	Tools	Objectives
1. Students of Business English are given instructions for a group-based project. They have to create a scenario requiring them to work together to suggest ways in which a company, which is on the verge of bankruptcy, can escape this difficult situation.	• Google Classroom (the LMS on which the assignment is posted)	Students: ➢ are introduced to the project. ➢ are familiarised with the evaluation criteria.
2. The students study the financials, do research and start brainstorming collaboratively in groups.	• Google Chrome (for research) • Jamboard (for brainstorming)	Students develop: ➢ research and critical thinking skills. ➢ communication skills
3. Students prepare a presentation in which they incorporate their ideas and suggestions on actions the company needs to take in order to solve the problems they are facing.	• Google Slides (for presentation) • Google docs (for notetaking) • Google Classroom (for submission of presentations)	Students develop: ➢ their writing skills ➢ public speaking skills. ➢ their vocabulary.

(Continued)

Steps	Tools	Objectives
4. The students also produce related written reports which they have to send to the board of directors of the company	• Google docs (for report writing) • Google Classroom (for submission of reports)	Students develop: ➢ their report writing skills.

Table 1: Example of PBLL in an ESP context through the use of Google Workspace for Education tools.

Table 2 describes ways in which some of the most important Google Workspace for Education tools can be used in ESP contexts to promote transversal competencies and create the potential for the development of autonomous and lifelong learning skills.

Google Workspace for Education tools	Practical suggestions for use in ESP contexts
Google Classroom	• Management of ESP coursework • Organisation of assignments and materials • Posting of announcements • Communication (Emails, sharing posts, commenting on posts)
Google Docs	• Collaborative synchronous and asynchronous writing on ESP topics with options for spell and grammar checking, dictionary, translation and voice typing • Use of Suggesting mode and Comments by course instructor and peers for feedback • Online chat • Possibility to see version history

(Continued)

Google Workspace for Education tools	Practical suggestions for use in ESP contexts
Google Slides	• Collaborative synchronous and asynchronous creation of slides for the delivery or oral presentations on ESP topics with options for spell checking and dictionary • Voice typing of speaker notes
Google Sheets	• Collaborative synchronous and asynchronous creation of sheets with spell checking • Possibility to see version history • Measurement of student progress and quick visualisation of results for the instructor
Google Meet	• Real-time visual or audio virtual communication between instructors and students or students themselves in an ESP class • Real-time student collaboration and discussion • Real-time provision of audio-visual feedback by instructor and peers
Google Forms	• Building of surveys for ESP course evaluation • Measurement of student success • Administration of quizzes
Google Sites	• Creation of English class sites related to students' specific discipline • Creation of students' e-portfolios
Google Chrome	• Searching for ESP audio-visual and written material • Researching databases in English related to students' specific discipline

Table 2: Practical suggestions for the use of Google Workspace for Education in ESP contexts.

The exploitation of these tools in ESP language classes, and the employment of new cloud technologies in general, can foster learner autonomy as well as other skills by providing learners with easy access to a range of resources, tools and environments for out-of-class learning experiences (Hafner & Miller, 2011). So, too, apart from enhancing the effectiveness of the teaching and learning process, such tools also help in the increase and improvement of students' responsibility and autonomy levels and study motivation (Borova et.al., 2021).

Conclusion

The need for the development of competencies and skills beyond the classroom has been generally recognised and acknowledged by the European Union and UNESCO and constitutes the focus of discussions on educational issues in many parts of the world. To achieve this goal, Higher Education should aim at developing such competencies and autonomous learning skills so that future graduates are equipped with the necessary qualifications to succeed in their professional and personal life. As part of Higher Education, ESP courses are particularly well suited to contribute to this endeavour through the development of learners' language skills, with specific focus on their field of study.

This paper aimed at providing readers with insights on the importance of transversal competencies and autonomous learning skills and making suggestions on how this can be achieved in ESP contexts. To develop language learners' transversal skills, Project-Based Language Learning (PBLL) is suggested, making projects professionally and personally relevant. Teachers guide the initial stages, suggesting resources but allowing student initiative. Trough an iterative project-based approach, collaboration, critical thinking, creativity, and engagement can be fostered, ultimately promoting learner autonomy and lifelong learning. Particular focus is placed on how transversal skills and independent learning habits can be developed through the use of cloud technologies. It discusses the different features of Google Workspace for Education and suggests ways in which different Google tools can be utilised in ESP contexts for the fostering of transversal skills and autonomous learning that may eventually lead to the development of a lifelong learning mindset.

References

Almendo, T. (2020). Challenging Efl Students To Read : Digital Reader Response Tasks To Foster Learner. *Teaching English with Technology*, Vol. 20, Issue 2: 21–41.

Aubrey, S. (2022). Enhancing long-term learner engagement through project-based learning. *ELT Journal*, Vol. 76, Issue 4: 441–451.

Barančicová, J., & Zerzová, J. (2015). English as a lingua franca used at international meetings. *Journal of Language and Cultural Education*, 3(3), 30–51.

Bell, S. (2010). Project-based learning for the 21st century: Skills for the future. *The Clearing House*, Vol. 83 (2), pp. 39–43. DOI: https://doi.org/10.1080/00098650903505415

Benadla, D., & Hadji, M. (2021). Arab World English Journal (AWEJ) Special Issue on Covid 19 Challenges April 2021 222–234. *Arab World English Journal, April*, 55–67.

Borova, T., Chekhratova, O., Marchuk, A., Pohorielova, T., & Zakharova, A. (2021). Fostering Students' Responsibility and Learner Autonomy by Using Google Educational Tools. *Revista Românească Pentru Educatie Multidimensionala*, Vol. 13, Issue 3: 73–94. DOI: https://doi.org/10.18662/rrem/13.3/441

Bosmans, D., Casciotta, F., & Fivaz, V. (2023). The Autonomous Acquisition of Transversal Competencies by Primary School

Children through the Use of Pedagogical Scenarios. *Athens Journal of Education*: 187.

Casper, W. C. (2017). Teaching beyond the topic teaching teamwork skills in higher education. *Journal of Higher Education Theory and Practice, 17*(6), 53–63.

Centre for Responsive Schools, Inc (2018). Who's in Charge of Learning in Your Elementary Classroom/School? https://www.responsiveclassroom.org/wp-content/uploads/2018/10/Whos-in-Charge-of-Learning-in-Your-Elementary-Classroom-School-Handout.pdf

Chalikandy, M. A. (2013). A Comprehensive Method for Teaching English for Specific Purpose. *Arab World English Journal*, Vol. 4, Issue 4.

Dantes, G. R., Rinawati, N. K. A., Suwastini, N. K. A., & Artini, N. N. (2022). Vocational school students' perceptions of Google Classroom in full online learning at the beginning of the Covid-19 pandemic. *Jurnal Pendidikan Teknologi Dan Kejuruan, 19*(2), 86–94.

ECML (European Centre for Modern Languages) (2021). *Transversal Competences in Language Education*. https://www.ecml.at/Portals/1/6MTP/project-hilden/documents/ECML-Transversal-competences-think-tank-background-paper-EN.pdf

European Commission (2017). *European Union Education and Training. About Higher Education Policy 2017*. https://education.ec.europa.eu/education-levels/higher-education

Fadhlullah, A., & Ahmad, N. (2017). Thinking outside of the box: Determining students' level of critical thinking skills in teaching and learning. *Asian Journal of University Education (AJUE)*, Vol. 13, Issue 2: 51–70.

Fleisher, S. (2009). Book Review: Motivation and Self-Regulated Learning: Theory, Research, and Applications. Edited by D. H. Schunk & B. J. Zimmerman (Lawrence Erlbaum Associates, 2008). *International Journal for the Scholarship of Teaching and Learning*, Vol. 3, Issue 1: 37.

Google. (2023). *Google Workspace for Education Overview*. https://support.google.com/a/answer/7370133?hl=en

Graddol, D. (2000). *The future of English? A guide to forecasting the popularity of the English language in the 21st century.* London: The British Council.

Guven, Z. Z., & Valais, T. H. (2014). Project based learning: A constructive way toward learner autonomy. *International Journal of Languages' Education and Teaching, 2*(3), 182–193.

Hafner, C. A., & Miller, L. (2011). Fostering Learner Autonomy in English for Science. *Language Learning & Technology, 15*(3), 68–86.

Humeniuk, I., Mushenyk, I., Popel, N., & Kuntso, O. (2023). Strategies for effective communication in educational environment in wartime. *Engineering for Rural Development*, 22–28. DOI: https://doi.org/10.22616/ERDev.2023.22.TF004

Jaganathan, P., Pandian, A., & Subramaniam, I. (2014). Language Courses, Transversal Skills and Transdisciplinary Education: A Case Study in the Malaysian University. *International Journal of Education and Research*, Vol. 2, Issue 1.

Jiang, P., Akhter, S., Azizi, Z., Gheisari, A., & Kumar, T. (2022). Exploring the role of content and language integrated learning approach in developing transversal skills in university students with respect to the mediating role of emotional intelligence. *Frontiers in Psychology*, Vol. 13. DOI: https://doi.org/10.3389/fpsyg.2022.988494

Johnson, K. & Johnson, H. (1998). English for specific purposes (ESP). In Keith Johnson & Helen Johnson (Eds), *Encyclopedic dictionary of applied linguistics.* Oxford: Blackwell: 105–110.

Kakoulli Constantinou, E. (2018). Teaching in Clouds: Using the G Suite for Education for the Delivery of Two English for Academic Purposes Courses. *The Journal of Teaching English for Specific and Academic Purposes, 6*(2), 305–317. DOI: https://doi.org/10.22190/jtesap1802305c

Kokotsaki, D., Menzies, V. and Wiggins, A. (2016). Project-based learning: A review of the literature. *Improving Schools*, Vol. 19 (3), pp. 267–277, Nov. 2016. DOI: https://doi.org/10.1177/1365480216659733

Lakshminarayanan, R., Kumar, B., & Raju, M. (2013). Cloud Computing Benefits for Educational Institutions. *Second International Conference of the Omani Society for Educational Technology,* 8(2), 104–112. http://arxiv.org/ftp/arxiv/papers/1305/1305.2616.pdf

Majid, S., Liming, Z., Tong, S., & Raihana, S. (2012). Importance of soft skills for education and career success. *International Journal for Cross-Disciplinary Subjects in Education,* 2(2), 1037–1042.

Mishra, K. (2014). Employability Skills That Recruiters Demand. *IUP Journal of Soft Skills,* 8(3).

Mystkowska-Wiertelak, A. (2022). Teachers' accounts of learners' engagement and disaffection in the language classroom. *The Language Learning Journal,* Vol. 50, Issue 3: 393–405.

National Institute of Standards and Technology (2021). *Cloud Computing.* https://csrc.nist.gov/projects/cloud-computing

Pokrovska, I. L., Kolodko, T. M., Aliyeva, Z. K., Tymoshchuk, I. V., & Vakariuk, R. V. (2020). Integration of cloud technologies in teaching foreign languages in higher education institutions. *International Journal of Learning, Teaching and Educational Research,* Vol. 19, Issue 2: 46–59. DOI: https://doi.org/10.26803/ijlter.19.2.4

Prastiwi, C. H. W., Rukmini, D., Saleh, M., & Astuti, P. (2021). Teaching 21st Century Skills to Engineering Students Through Project-Based Learning (Social Semiotic Perspective). In *6th International Conference on Science, Education and Technology (ISET 2020)* (pp. 313–319). Atlantis Press.

Rahman, M. (2015). *English for Specific Purposes (ESP): A Holistic Review.* Universal Journal of Educational Research.

Richardson, V. (1997). 'Constructivist Teaching and Teacher Education: Theory and Practice', in Richardson, V. (ed.) *Constructivist Teacher Education: Building a World of New Understandings.* London: Falmer Press, pp. 3–14.

Rodríguez-Peñarroja, M. (2022). Integrating project-based learning, task-based language teaching approach and Youtube in the ESP class: A study on students' motivation. *Teaching English with Technology,* Vol. 22 (1), pp. 62–81.

Siemens, G. (2004). Elearnspace. Connectivism: A learning theory for the digital age. *Elearnspace.org*, 14–16.

Sinkus, T. (2020). Development of Transversal Competences in Case Study-based Professional English Course in Business Administration Studies. In *The Proceedings of the International Scientific Conference Rural Environment. Education. Personality (REEP)*. Vol. 13: 142–149.

Socciarelli, M., Takeuchi, A., & Müller, I. M. G. (2020). Developing learners' critical thinking skills by exploring social issues in Project-Based Language Learning: Three proposals. *TESOL Working Paper Series*, Vol. 18: 18–57.

Sultan, N. (2010). Cloud computing for education: A new dawn? *International Journal of Information Management*, 30(2), 109–116. DOI: https://doi.org/10.1016/j.ijinfomgt.2009.09.004

Susilawati, S. (2023). Integrating Content and Language to Teach ESP Writing Online with the Assistance of Google Docs. *Journal of Languages and Language Teaching*, 11(1), 14–26. DOI: https://doi.org/10.33394/jollt.v11i1.6617

Thuan, P. D. (2018). Project-based learning: From theory to EFL classroom practice. In *Proceedings of the 6th International OpenTESOL Conference*, Vol. 327.

Tuyen, L.V. & Tien, H.H. (2021). Integrating Project-Based Learning into English for Specific Purposes Classes at Tertiary Level: Perceived Challenges and Benefits. *VNU Journal of Foreign Studies*, Vol. 37 (4).

UNESCO IBE (2013). *IBE Glossary of Curriculum Terminology*. https://www.ibe.unesco.org/sites/default/files/resources/ibe-glossary-curriculum.pdf

UNESCO Office Bangkok and Regional Bureau for Education in Asia and the Pacific (2015). *Transversal Competencies in Education Policy and Practice (Phase I)*. 2013 Asia-Pacific Education Research Institutes Network (ERI-NET). Paris and Bangkok, UNESCO. http://unesdoc.unesco.org/images/0023/002319/231907E.pdf

UNESCO Office Bangkok and Regional Bureau for Education in Asia and the Pacific (2016). *School and teaching practices for twenty-first century challenges: lessons from the Asia-Pacific region, regional synthesis report; 2014 regional study on transversal competencies in education policy and practice (Phase II).* Paris and Bangkok, UNESCO. https://unesdoc.unesco.org/ark:/48223/pf0000244022

UNESCO Institute for Lifelong Learning (2020). *National Lifelong Learning Strategy 2014–2020.* https://www.uil.unesco.org/en/articles/cyprus-national-lifelong-learning-strategy-2020-issued-2014

Xie, Y., Ryder, L., & Chen, Y. (2019). Using Interactive Virtual Reality Tools in an Advanced Chinese Language Class: a Case Study. *TechTrends*: 251–259. DOI: https://doi.org/10.1007/s11528-019-00389-z

Yi-Ping Huang (2018). Learner Resistance to English-medium instruction practices: a qualitative case study. In *Teaching in Higher Education*, Vol. 23, Issue 4: 435–449, DOI: https://doi.org/10.1080/13562517.2017.1421629

Multimodal Reflective Journals and Life Writing: A Didactic Approach to Enhanced Learning

Dana Di Pardo Léon-Henri
ELLIADD, University of Besancon Franche-Comté, France
danaleonhenri@gmail.com

Abstract

This research investigates how self-reflection, journaling, and life writing can foster significant educational and personal growth among tertiary-level students with a focus on the tumultuous period of the Covid-19 pandemic. It explores the transformative power of these methodologies in developing metacognitive skills, soft skills, and self-regulation abilities essential for students navigating contemporary challenges exacerbated by rapid technological advancements

---

How to cite this book chapter:
Di Pardo Léon-Henri, D. 2024. Multimodal Reflective Journals and Life Writing: A Didactic Approach to Enhanced Learning. In: Athanasiou, A., Hadjiconstantinou, S. and Christoforou, M. (Eds.) *Innovative Language Teaching Practices in Higher Education in a Post-COVID Era*. Pp. 49–71. London: Ubiquity Press. DOI: https://doi.org/10.5334/bdd.d. License: CC BY 4.0

and social shifts. Utilizing a multimodal approach, students engaged in reflective writing exercises incorporating text, drawings, photography, and other media forms, revealing diverse coping mechanisms and enhanced self-awareness.

The data, drawn from anonymous student journal excerpts from 2020–2021 and 2021–2022, underscores the benefits of reflective journaling in promoting emotional resilience, intercultural awareness, and improved cognitive processes. Through detailed qualitative analysis, the study illustrates the profound impact of life writing on students' self-perception, academic performance, and overall well-being. It reveals how these practices enhance students' abilities to process complex emotions and situations, fostering a deeper understanding of themselves and their environments. The findings advocate for the integration of reflective journaling and life writing into educational practices to better prepare students for the evolving demands of the global job market and personal life challenges, highlighting their role in developing a versatile, resilient, and self-aware individual.

Introduction

Technology's rapid evolution and global interconnectedness have fundamentally reshaped societies. The onset of the Covid-19 pandemic in 2019 accelerated these transformations, disrupting norms and prompting profound shifts across personal, educational, and professional spheres worldwide. This crisis highlighted the critical importance of resilience and adaptability in the face of unprecedented challenges, fundamentally reshaping perspectives on work-life balance and career trajectories. Educational institutions swiftly adapted to remote learning during the pandemic, revealing disparities in technology access and necessitating a reassessment of teaching methodologies.

For educators, these shifts significantly altered teaching and learning practices, emphasizing the shared responsibility between teachers and students in achieving common educational objectives (European Commission, 2013). Educational settings became crucial arenas for cultivating skills that foster independence and resilience. The pandemic, coupled with ongoing technological advancements, has rapidly transformed the job market (Organisation for Economic Co-operation and Development, 2021), necessitating the development of effective strategies to navigate personal and professional pressures. Key among these are metacognitive skills, soft skills such as communication and adaptability, and self-regulation abilities, all vital throughout an individual's lifetime.

In an increasingly interconnected world, cultural capital has gained prominence, with reflective journals and life writing serving as powerful tools for students to explore personal narratives and cultural identities. These practices not only enhance language proficiency and communication skills but also cultivate empathy and foster intercultural understanding. This paper explores how reflective journaling and life writing are pivotal in transforming tertiary education, especially in the post-pandemic era. By examining their impact on metacognitive development, acquisition of soft skills, and enhancement of self-awareness and self-regulation, this study illuminates their role in fostering holistic student growth. Through qualitative inquiry and educational theory, it underscores their pedagogical value in preparing graduates for diverse professional environments.

Contextual Framework

Technological advances and increased international mobility have provided the momentum for remarkable change on many levels in our societies. However, the Covid-19 pandemic in 2019 and 2020 abruptly halted cities and catalyzed significant social transformations marked by uncertainty, stress, and fear. Distance learning exacerbated inequalities based on technological access, reshaping global job markets with a shift to soft skills, AI-driven job replacement, and demands for flexibility, reflecting ongoing re-evaluations of societal roles (Organisation for Economic Co-operation and Development, 2021).

During this unprecedented worldwide event, many individuals took the time to reassess their life/work balance. Simultaneously, this occurrence bolstered world job markets. On an international scale, transformations accelerated on differing levels pertaining to professional skill requirements (shifting from hard to soft skills), diminishing job opportunities since many jobs are being replaced by technology or artificial intelligence (AI), and candidate flexibility demands (nomad status or working from home, higher wages, improved quality of life). Today, this trend continues to accelerate as the impact of the place we occupy in this world is under scrutiny and constant revaluation. Highly concerned by the global and environmental situation, tertiary-level students continue to navigate these turbulent waters. Widespread anxieties persist and remain relatively high as students wonder about looming professional career choices increasingly impacted by the influence of AI-related technologies.

Educators faced paradigm shifts in teaching methods during Covid-19, necessitating adaptability in both pre-pandemic and post-pandemic educational contexts (European Commission,

2013). This period highlighted the shared responsibility of teachers and students in achieving educational objectives, fostering independence, and resilience amid rapid technological advancements and job market volatility (Schwab, 2016; Gamota, 2020).

As societies evolve amidst technological dependencies and pandemic influences, the job landscape continues to transform (Organisation for Economic Co-operation and Development, 2021), necessitating skills in metacognition, soft skills, and self-regulation (Brown et al., 1983; Gray, 2016). These skills are crucial for navigating personal and professional challenges, emphasizing the need for strategic development and adaptability in an uncertain global environment. To better ascertain these skills, it is fundamental to first define, then illustrate each group.

Transversal Life Skills

Understanding how our own cognitive process functions is beneficial in understanding how others function, particularly in teamwork and social activities. Metacognitive knowledge helps individuals grasp their own and others' cognitive processes (Flavell and Wellman, 1977). Acquired formally or informally, these skills are transferable and transversal (Flavell, 1979). Metacognitive awareness allows individuals to recognize and articulate their knowledge and understanding (Brown et al., 1983). They evolve with personal and professional experience and potentially improve through social interaction and knowledge. Schraw and Dennison (1994) offer insights into techniques for assessing students' metacognitive skills, while Wenden (1998) examines their role in language learning. Oxford (2011) provides practical methods for integrating metacognitive instruction into language teaching. Classroom techniques can also enhance listening comprehension and communication skills (Vandergrift and Goh, 2012) during debates and discussions. Reflective journals prompt students to examine their critical thinking, decision-making, and problem-solving approaches, fostering a heightened awareness of these cognitive abilities. A veritable superpower, this heightened awareness can be a powerful tool to improve overall communication skills.

Soft skills enable individuals to effectively interact, communicate, and eventually collaborate with others. Cherished by employers, these transversal skills include (verbal and non-verbal) communication, collaboration or teamwork, adaptability, critical thinking, interpersonal skills, problem-solving, empathy, leadership, time management, conflict resolution, networking, cultural awareness, and innovation or creativity. The value attributed to each of these transversal soft skills will evolve with time, since AI and technology in the workplace is undergoing constant and rapid change (Gray, 2016). During Covid-19, the need to self-isolate and remain at or work from home became a massive challenge for some, while others flourished and welcomed the opportunity. Support and guidance were often provided to individuals (students or employees) who needed to quickly adapt to and learn more about technology. Those who often flourished during this global medical crisis were the autonomous self-taught learners. Possessing these transversal soft skills clearly made the difference, as did the ability to adapt and manage one's productivity, emotions, and stress levels which brings us to the next group of significant skills.

Self or auto-regulation skills are significant since they refer to the ability to manage or control one's thoughts, emotions, and behaviors to better adapt to situations, while remaining focused on achieving one's desired objectives. A complex group of skills influencing a wide range of behaviours, they involve being aware of one's own internal (emotional or psychological) states (Carver and Scheier, 1998). Emotional intelligence and regulation (feeling management and emotional responses), impulse control (resisting urges and maintaining self-control), self-discipline (setting goals and prioritizing), cognitive control (concentration and memory), stress management (relaxation and strategies to manage stress), and self-monitoring (observing and evaluating one's actions, thoughts, and behaviors, often through reflection and self-assessment) are also affected by self-regulation. These skills play a crucial role in many areas of our lives: from interpersonal relationships, academic, professional success, to overall self-development (Gross, 1998).

Reflective Journals and Life Writing

From a sociolinguistic perspective, each language learning environment is a unique context since it can serve as a forum for constructing and reconstructing or reproducing idealizations of one's own intercultural spaces (Duff, 2015). These idealizations can symbolize cultural capital. As Barnawi (2017) and McNamara (2010) postulate, English language assessment practices are social activities in transnational spaces, and the ways in which students are being assessed in social and educational contexts reflect how they are seen, positioned, and accommodated by their institutions. Their voice and concerns should therefore find a place for expression. An opportunity for enhanced learning and the construction of cultural capital, reflective journals are a means to encourage students to reflect on and renew with the pleasure of writing and expressing one's inner voice. Autobiographical writing englobes reflective journals and life writing. A prominent French specialist in this field Philippe Lejeune has had an indelible mark on the development of autobiography pedagogy and the application of life writing in educational contexts. Lejeune (1989; 1996) presents a comprehensive overview and theoretical framework for exploring, theorizing, and understanding this genre. Self-representation, identity construction, and the zones between truth and fiction are the focus of his life's work (Lejeune, 2008; 2015). Before presenting the methodology for this study, it is important to initially understand the characteristics of life writing.

Life writing refers to the genre of literature that encompasses personal reflections, accounts, or narratives about one's own life experiences. Regardless of its form, life writing is a student-centered approach that encourages learners to develop a 'can-do' attitude, which is effective, motivating, and enjoyable for both students and teachers (Jones, 2007). Smith & Watson (1996) explore key concepts related to life writing within the context of literary theory, providing critical analysis and interpretation methods. This genre can take various forms, such as diaries, letters, (travel) journals, personal essays, vlogs, blogs, memoirs, or autobiographical novels, and it has existed across cultures. Some examples include encrypted historical archives (Whitbread, 1992) or light-hearted fun (Fielding, 2013).

Life writing and the diary share similarities in that they involve personal accounts and reflections on life experiences. However, they differ in scope and intent. A diary, often private, is typically a daily or regular record of events, thoughts, and feelings, intended for personal use. In contrast, life writing has a broader scope and often aims to explore themes and convey a deeper sense of life's meaning. While a diary tends to be spontaneous and chronological, life writing can be more refined and destined for publication. Analysis of these forms reveals various expressions of self, including identity, intercultural communication, and reminiscence.

A dynamic mechanism and inherently multimodal, life writing invites creativity and innovation through various forms and media. Expressing insights and social interactions with others, they are windows into what makes us tick and how society functions. From diachronic or synchronic perspectives, these practical record-keeping tools also provide valuable insights into the unique cultural viewpoints or perspectives, ideologies, and philosophies on life. Building bridges of understanding between increasingly diverse populations, life writing is the articulation of lived experiences, ideas, values, and feelings (Hasebe-Ludt, 2014). Students who practice this form of literature gain a deeper perception of their own identity, while developing an inherent appreciation and heightened level of respect towards others.

Methodological Framework

This Languages for Specific Purpose (LSP) literature class for non-specialists of English[1] was composed of approximately 35 first year Master (M1) students from differing disciplines (philosophy, sociology, children's literature, etc.). The anonymous journal excerpts from this task-based multi-modal reflective life writing activity were taken from 2020–2021 and 2021–2022.

Students were encouraged to reflect and express their thoughts in English using either modern technology (computers) or traditional methods (notebooks and writing instruments). There

---

[1] Based on life writing as a literary genre. For full course details, refer to Di Pardo Léon-Henri (2020).

was no word limit to avoid influencing their personal investment and creativity. They were also encouraged to adopt a multi-modal approach, incorporating various media and art forms such as drawings, word clouds, paintings, photography, video, sculpture, and collage. All combinations of media were welcomed and appreciated to make their work unique and personal.

Results

Corpus A: (Autumn 2021, three of 35 students or 11% of the total number of enrolled students)

Three participating female students[2] M1 (Humanities) all French origin in differing fields:

Modern Literature (student referred to as [MG]), Antiquity Studies (EP), Theatre Studies (AB).

Their approach to this activity was substantially different. While all three used various techniques, such as words and paragraphs, poetry, drawings, photography, pictograms, and montage, one student decided to include paintings of her feelings in *aquarelle*. Submitted on the Moodle platform in .pdf format, hand drawn or painted artistic work was first photographed and then integrated into the .pdf document.

With black and white scribble-type drawings, MG provides a title and descriptive initial backdrop. She provides daily entries; however, on many days a drawing or short poem replaces text. Revealing a true penchant to join the rank of author, she states: 'My very first bestseller." She also reveals a few marketing skills for a creative and exciting read:

---

[2] Names will be replaced by their initials to protect the student's anonymity.

Covid Diary
My very first bestseller (without any undue ego on my part), which I will call: *"Journal d'une Exilée Covidée"*[3]. I promise you many epic twists and turns... I will be the only character... A full dive into what has been called the "stream of consciousness". A scenario voluntarily reduced to a closed space, namely the four walls of my room... A sort of contemporary rewriting of Robinson Crusoe, the exotic and wild setting in less.... although with the legion of microbes that plague my inhospitable environment, one could quickly create a parallel between my room and a hostile jungle.

With a Robinson Crusoe reference, she beckons the call of adventure and employs words that intrigue ("exotic and wild"). The author's humorous, sardonic tone is expressed with the "four walls of my room" and the Covid reference "the legion of microbes that plague my inhospitable environment." Tinged with a strong militant undertone MG, uses humour to describe and explain her frustrations, as well as her overall stance on the vaccination program that was highly promoted and enforced at that time:

Day 2: Sunday 14th of November 2021
It seems that time passes. Slowly, but, as a matter of fact, it passes. I still don't realize the verdict that fell yesterday morning, at 11:39 am, precisely (since it is specified on the result of my "swirling cotton swab nostril rape" test). "I keep in memory the serious and concerned features of this pharmacist, who must have been thinking: "another big anti-vax turkey who will inflate the statistics of our country in full sanitary decline... but go and get vaccinated". And the boy is probably right, yes, I am an egoist who refuses to submit to a simple collective and citizen

---

[3] English translation: "Diary of an Exiled Covid Victim".

> gesture, resulting from gene therapy, which would have certainly participated in saving lives and which would have been only a small step for me and a huge step for humanity. I could have felt invested with the divine mission to save the world, yes! But alas, I don't feel like a superhero, and I don't have any admissible argument to justify my unforgivable crime against humanity. So, I plead guilty, O Mister Pharmacist!
>
> And as a punishment for this sin of civil irresponsibility, here I am (again) locked up, confined for at least seven long and interminable days, having for doubtful company, only the presence of my own microbes that I will have soon affectionate as one affectionate one's captor in the case of a severe Stockholm syndrome.

Replete with many literary devices such as simile, metaphor, alliteration, etc., her words reveal the daily dilemmas many people faced during the pandemic. She shares the rationale behind her decisions while reflecting on the cause and effect of her situation. Resolutely opinionated, MG assumes her choices and shares the collective feelings of isolation that characterised this chaotic period.

Similarly, EP establishes her intent very early in "My Diary" with a very modest, discrete, and humble:

> I know that my diary is more like a story, but a diary is private, so I don't dare share all my feelings.

She continues with a structured, regular weekly installment which ironically occasionally goes against her original intentions as this entry shows:

> Week one
> September 27th to October 3rd
> Since the beginning of the school year, I'm a little bit sad. Why? Because I really feel alone. The three years

ago, I was ... [studying the Classics][4] ...with three close friends. But since the start of the academic year... I'm alone here. Another person joined me in Master, but [it] is not the same, I really feel alone. For the moment, I don't have a lot of courses, but I have a lot of homework.

EP illustrates her need for coping mechanisms, self-awareness, and self-regulation in her rationalizations and to fill the imposed void. Her texts are underscored by cartoons and soft-colored or faint *aquarelle*. Sharing her love of languages, she naturally gives way to her inner voice by relating her feelings, emotions, and investment:

Today, on Wednesday, September 29th, I had my first English class, and we will work on a diary. I love to learn new languages, but I must admit that I am not very good... So, for this course, we were offered a bonus activity, where we must write our diary. Since always, I love to write, and I often try to keep a diary, but I always abandoned by laziness or forgetfulness. So, this time, I will try to keep it up all semester, and more, it will be an occasion to be better in English and to improve my grades, that is perfect!

Punctuated by colourful photos of nature, birds, flowers, and monuments, her texts reveal a natural flow and ebb. She passes from one topic or event to another like when she explains a trip to an amusement park in Rust, Germany:

On Saturday, October 2nd, I went to Europa Park. ... I fell in love with this park. So, I try to go again regularly and nearly every year. I decided to go with my best friend,

---

[4] To improve overall flow, some grammatical corrections were necessary. However, every effort was taken to respect the original idea to avoid altering or interpreting the student's message.

Marianne, whom I have known since almost ten years! We had a lot of fun, but, because it was on a Saturday and the first day of Halloween decorations, there were a lot of people! We still had a good time and did all the attractions we wanted to do, and that's what matters! We came home really exhausted but happy…we don't see each other very often.

At the end of this passage, her emotions are present as she looks on the bright side (EP's dominant coping mechanism). Highly motivated and invested, she triumphantly explains that she successfully wrote every day for the full 10 weeks:

Week ten:
November 29th to December 5th
I finished my semester, and I'm so proud of myself because I did all my work and presentations on time, and my teachers were happy…, so I'm happy too! I was so glad to do this diary and I want to say that [I never] did a big work like that, and I did it – in English! When writing my words every day, I learned to think in English and not French first! Now, it's time to finish! Bye! Have a good day!

Enhanced learning, metacognitive skills development, and the reflective process involved in this activity are validated by this passage. EP shares the implicit/explicit pleasure of successfully having followed through with her initial declaration. The progression she makes is evident when she explains that she is now able to think and write without having to think about translating from her native language. A highly valuable time and learning investment in herself, this activity represents a personal achievement.

And finally, AB from Theatre Studies provided the most staggering, expansive (60 pages in all), and detailed document in this group. Her "Dear Diary" is full of insights, illustrations, and photos or drawings of famous theatre characters, as well as colourful Japanese *kabuki* photos. A long-term survivor battling with eating disorders, AB unfailingly writes about her relationship with food, yoga, and the way she perceives herself. She details her constant bouts of anxiety and regret after "eating too much" ("she says of an apple and two biscuits") and then purging ("the burning in my throat is the worst"). She writes about her medical team who sometimes trigger her destructive behaviour. One revealing insight into her metacognitive awareness is the passage from December 10, 2021, when AB explains:

> I'm still a bit sick. I'm doing much better but still a bit sick. Sometimes I feel like I'm never going to come out of this sickness. Plus, my body feels so heavy and stiff, it's aching. It's like my body is always sleepy, it can't wake or turn on. … Worked on my opera class and did yoga. I was not efficient at all on my opera studies. BECAUSE this lesson is starting to really make me angry. I feel like I'm learning it every day but the next day everything seems to have magically (notice the humour) disappear from my head. I don't understand how, but it happens. And it is really starting to annoy me…. So Good Night, dear diary. (I think I really like that expression "dear diary" I might use it some more).

The use of capital letters and undertones of sarcasm or quotation marks are common in her work, which is the most colourful (use of vivid and very contrasting colours) of this group.

Corpus B: (Autumn 2022, five of 35 students or 18% of the total number of enrolled students)

Four participating female students + 1 transgender student, all French origin

All five M1 (Humanities) studying Children's Literature (CA, JD, MP-T, LH, and AL-J)

Some diaries were relatively short (from six to ten pages or a very concise three pages [of one-line entries]. Four diaries were uploaded to Moodle in .pdf format. AL-J adopted a traditional approach by submitting an embossed hand-written (calligraphy style) journal containing 80 pages. Excerpts from the written production of only two of these students will be presented here.

With her title "Diary of my cumbersome thoughts" CA piques the reader's curiosity. Punctuated by differing fonts and letter styles, CA's work is as visually intriguing as her words. Sprinkled with naïve questions or statements, her texts are unique and reveal many coping mechanisms to deal with the turmoil of the times:

> Thursday October 6, 2022
> Hello! Sometimes, I think to myself than I shouldn't pull the skin off my fingers and drop them in the street. A scientist could pick them up and use them to make clones of myself. It would be annoying; I haven't given consent to this experiment. I wonder what it's like to have a clone of ourselves. It means someone we can send it to do the boring job for us.
>
> Monday October 10, 2022
> I still [do] not have a clone. I must admit I'm a bit disappointed.
>
> Thursday October 20, 2022
> Today I talked to AM [an Italian ERASMUS student] about pizza in Italy. So many funny gestures! She was saying, "Pizza in France is not pizza." (French gestures are weird too). AM said in France we only have maybe 10 or 20 pizzas at the most. When I said that I like "Margherita", she laughed at me. She told me that where she

> comes from you can have any pizza or pasta you want. She's making *tiramisu* for us at the end of the semester. A real one. I can't wait to taste it. My clone is not getting any, but I still don't have one.

Unconscious nervous habits and inner conversations are her focus. Through interactions with an ERASMUS participant (AM) from Italy, AM provides clear insights into intercultural awareness, gestures, and Italian perspectives on French cuisine. Framed with humorous illustrations, the text also includes word clouds or poetry. The following is amongst the entries of mid-November:

> I'm sick, I'm cold, I'm tired, I'm hungry.
> I had to eat "healthy" (because last week was not "healthy" (sandwich, burgers (twice).)
> I'm at the library but people are talking loudly.
> What a beautiful *haiku*!
>   Sounds like *ahhhh chooo*!

An illustration of metacognitive awareness and auto-regulation (taking control, eating healthier), the text illustrates rudimentary student needs and feelings. And yet, although CA appears to be ill, she takes the time to admire her "beautiful" poetic creation.

Finally, MP-T discloses painful insights, like the meticulously structured (date, title, paragraph) passages below illustrate:

> October 16th, 2022, 9:15 PM
> How? Much? More? Time?
> Friday, I saw my psychologist and Saturday my psychiatrist, the two specialists who are supposed to be there to help me get better, but I still feel much too bad. My psychologist told me that it's normal that I feel in this kind of blurred bubble, indescribable, of unreality, as if I was living a life that wasn't mine, someone else's life. Apparently, I need to take time for myself, do things I love, go

out with friends, have fun, breathe, and that it's normal to have this fling and that it would take time. How much more time?

October 18th, 2022, 8:15 PM
Alone.
I still feel terrible about myself and my mind, I saw my psychologist and psychiatrist this week and I feel incredibly alone and misunderstood … I just don't know what I feel. I don't know who I am or what I'm worth.

November 4th, 2022, 8:30 PM,
Thoughts. Thinking. Reflection.
I am always in my head, and it gets worse and worse. The transition between teenager and adult is scaring me. I dislike reality, I prefer to take refuge in my head, in my world but I am also ashamed. Why can't I live like everyone? At the same time, I feel safe in my head, I had the control of what happened or not.

These passages reveal a coping mechanism and the profound need to channel the chaos of her feelings through this diary. Her observations uncover the fear and apprehension associated with assuming responsibilities and becoming an adult. Taking refuge "in [her] head, in [her] world" is her attempt at an autoregulative coping strategy.

Discussion

Promoting and advocating students' reflective writing underscores its value as a beneficial practice for fostering reflection and self-management. Although there was a slight increase in participants in the second year, the participant count remains relatively low, likely since the assignment is an extra credit activity at the graduate level where many students must prioritize their time. This activity provides a forum for students to share their inner voice and viewpoints, aligning with the conceptual framework that emphasizes personal and professional skill development in a rapidly changing society (Organisation for Economic Co-operation and Development, 2021). Special attention must be given to the precise formulation of the activity itself to avoid directly influencing or limiting student expression, promoting metacognitive awareness (Flavell and Wellman, 1977; Brown et al., 1983) and enhancing soft skills (Gray, 2016).

To encourage a multimodal and creative dimension, every effort should embrace all forms of artistic freedom. While language correction was not the goal, as students were freed from the constraint of writing perfectly constructed texts, assessment presented a challenge. This approach provided an outlet for students to freely compose and reconnect with language, fostering self-regulation abilities (Carver and Scheier, 1998). Few grammatical errors existed; overall language quality was remarkably good for these motivated non-specialist students. Supportive, non-critical feedback was provided on an individual basis outside of classroom time to respect privacy. When applicable, students were encouraged to continue writing outside of the class and seek professional guidance if needed.

This activity supports the development of metacognitive skills, soft skills, and self-regulation, crucial for navigating the evolving job landscape (Gamota, 2020). Every effort was made to provide an unbiased, comprehensive assessment encompassing writing quality, literary techniques, expressive styles, and the multimodal aspects. Since this literature course values life writing, each participating student received a 3-point credit on their overall participation grade. They were encouraged to treasure their diary as a historical marker of this special time in their life for future reading or sharing.

Conclusion

This genre has illustrated the firsthand benefits of soft skills building to cope with chaos during, throughout, and post-Covid. By contemplating, dealing with, and sharing their daily trials and tribulations, the students were also able to develop and strengthen their metacognitive skills. A true window into the lives of these students, this unpretentious but highly effective form of writing encapsulates a myriad of topics, perspectives, and cultural insights (for instance, Italian and French intercultural perceptions). The corpus presented here illustrates student engagement in foreign language expression, as well as the expression of their ideologies and life philosophies during an unprecedented pandemic. Revealing many traces of metacognitive awareness and enhanced learning, the corpus comprises cultural capital that provides snapshots of daily experiences, while encoding perspectives on "routine" social or cultural interactions.

Future improvements to this didactic approach may focus on encouraging greater student participation and investment. One approach might be to make it compulsory. However, that may prove counterproductive since the intention is to offer an optional activity that is intrinsically/extrinsically motivating to reflect on life, decompress, inspire, and creatively imagine. Further research studies might include AI-based tools for correction and AI-based text-to-image technology for the artistic dimension. Multimodal reflective journals that include artistic and intercultural dimensions can be applied to various plurilingual learning settings with students of all ages (from young to adult or lifelong learners). Adaptable to all ([foreign] language) teaching environments, this didactic approach serves as an opportunity for learners to focus on and synthesize daily activities while developing their metacognitive, soft, and self-regulation skills. Additionally, it offers them the innovative and imaginative freedom to self-invest while encapsulating (inter)cultural capital. Finally, it encourages students to break free from their daily routine to live in the moment and reflect on the true meaning of life. Some may mistakenly call this the humdrum happenings of everyday life, while others view these precious and unique moments as part of the journey and valuable life lessons.

References

Barnawi, O. (2017). English language assessment: Global perspectives, local practices. *Language Testing in Asia, 7*(3), Article 10.

Brown, A., J. D. Bransford, R. Ferrara & J. C. Campione Lael. (1983). "Learning, remembering and understanding," in J. H. Flavell & E. M. Markman (Eds.), *Carmichael's Manual of Child Psychology Volume 1*. New York: Wiley.

European Commission. (2013). *High level group on the modernisation of higher education. Report to the European Commission on improving the quality of teaching and learning in Europe's higher education institutions.* Publications Office of the European Union. https://publications.europa.eu/en/publication-detail/-/publication/fbd4c2aa-aeb7-41acab4c-a94feea9eb1f

Carver, C. S., & Scheier, M. F. (1998). *On the self-regulation of behavior*. Cambridge: Cambridge University Press.

Di Pardo Léon-Henri, D. (2020). "Teaching Communication Skills through Literature: Encouraging Master's Level ESP Students to Speak Up and Move," in Di Pardo Léon-Henri, D. & Jain, B. (Eds.), *Contemporary Research in Foreign Language*

Teaching and Learning, Newcastle upon Tyne: Cambridge Scholars Publishing, 80–105.

Duff, P. (2015). Transnationalism, Multilingualism, and Identity. *Annual Review of Applied Linguistics*, 35, 57–80. DOI: https://doi.org/10.1017/S026719051400018X

Fielding, H. (2013). *Bridget Jones: Mad About the Boy*. London: Jonathan Cape Ltd.

Flavell, J. H. (1979). Metacognition and cognitive monitoring: A new area of cognitive-developmental inquiry. *American Psychologist, 34*(10), 906–911.

Flavell, J. & H. M. Wellmann. (1977). 'Metamemory' in R. V. Kail, Jr & J. W. Hagen (Eds.), *Perspectives on the Development of Memory and Cognition*. Hillsdale N.J.: Lawrence Erlbaum Associates.

Gamota, D. (2020, Dec. 28). How Covid-19 Is Driving the Evolution of Industry 5.0. *Forbes*. https://www.forbes.com/sites/forbestechcouncil/2021/12/28/how-covid-19-is-driving-the-evolution-of-industry-50/?sh=4a89e5cc2062

Gray, A. (2016, Jan 19). The 10 skills you need to thrive in the fourth industrial revolution. *World Economic Forum*. https://www.weforum.org/agenda/2016/01/the-10-skills-youneed-to-thrive-in-the-fourth-industrial-revolution/

Gross, J. J. (1998). The emerging field of emotion regulation: An integrative review. *Review of General Psychology, 2*(3), 271–299.

Hasebe-Ludt, E. (2014). Life writing as literacy: Teaching and learning discourse across cultures. *Language and Education, 28*(1), 61–77.

Jones, L. (2007). *The student-centred classroom*. Cambridge: Cambridge University Press.

Lejeune, P. (1989). *On Autobiography*. Minneapolis: University of Minnesota Press.

Lejeune, P. (1996). The Autobiographical Pact. In S. Smith & J. Watson (Eds.), *Getting a Life: Everyday Uses of Autobiography* (3–30). Minneapolis: University of Minnesota Press.

Lejeune, P. (2008). *On Diary*. Honolulu: University of Hawai'i Press.

Lejeune, P. (2015). *Cher écran : Journal personnel, ordinateur, internet*. Paris: Seuil.

McNamara, T. (2010). Language testing: The social dimension. *MEXTESOL Journal, 34*(2), 1–14.

Organisation for Economic Co-operation and Development [OECD] (2021, Apr. 9). *An assessment of the impact of COVID-19 on job and skills demand using online job vacancy data*. https://www.oecd.org/coronavirus/policy-responses/an-assessment-of-the-impact-of-covid-19-on-job-and-skills-demand-using-online-job-vacancy-data-20fff09e/

Oxford, R. L. (2011). *Teaching and researching language learning strategies*. London: Routledge.

Schwab, K. (2016, Jan 14). The fourth industrial revolution: what it means, how to respond. *World Economic Forum*. https://www.weforum.org/agenda/2016/01/the-fourth-industrial-revolution-what-it-means-and-how-to-respond/

Schraw, G. & Dennison, R. S. (1994). Assessing metacognitive awareness. *Contemporary Educational Psychology, 19*(4), 460–475.

Smith, S. & J. Watson (1996). *Getting a Life: Everyday Uses of Autobiography*. Minneapolis: University of Minnesota Press.

Vandergrift, L., & Goh, C. C. M. (2012). *Teaching and learning second language listening: Metacognition in action*. New York: Routledge.

Wenden, A. L. (1998). Metacognitive knowledge and language learning. *Applied Linguistics, 19*(4), 515–537.

Whitbread, H. (1992). *I Know My Own Heart: The Diaries of Anne Lister 1791–1840*. New York: New York Press.

Online Practices for Teaching English Grammar in Higher Education: Combining the flipped classroom with digital learning paths

Eirini Busack
Karlsruhe University of Education, Germany
eirinibusack@gmail.com

Abstract

This study investigates whether the combination of digital learning paths (DLPs) and the flipped classroom can help pre-service English teachers improve their grammar and meet the communication and social needs of the post-COVID era. To answer the question, the seminar "Development of media-didactic competencies: Learning Paths & Digital Storytelling for Teaching English Grammar"

How to cite this book chapter:
Busack, E. 2024. Online Practices for Teaching English Grammar in Higher Education: Combining the flipped classroom with digital learning paths. In: Athanasiou, A., Hadjiconstantinou, S. and Christoforou, M. (Eds.) *Innovative Language Teaching Practices in Higher Education in a Post-COVID Era*. Pp. 73–96. London: Ubiquity Press. DOI: https://doi.org/10.5334/bdd.e. License: CC BY 4.0

was offered as a flipped classroom with a synchronous part (webinar) and an asynchronous courseware part in the form of DLPs. Data were collected on the extent to which the combination of DLPs and the flipped classroom helped pre-service English teachers improve their grammar and meet the communication and social needs of the post-pandemic era through an online post-grammar test and an online course evaluation survey at the end of the seminar. The results showed that 100% of participants improved their grammar knowledge and 87% confirmed that they had benefited from a seminar that involved continuous reflection and a plausible relationship between technology and pedagogy. The results of this study will encourage instructors to use the combination of DLP and webinars to enhance their teaching whenever classroom teaching is impossible.

Introduction

As a result of the COVID-19 pandemic, educational institutions at all levels have had to make significant adjustments to their learning, teaching, and assessment methods to adapt to the rapidly changing circumstances. In the realm of Higher Education (HE), a staggering 95% of universities in Europe had implemented lockdown measures and swiftly transitioned to online teaching by the end of March 2020 (European University Association, 2020). A considerable number of language teacher trainers were directed to adopt a fully asynchronous approach to instruction. This involved uploading learning materials and pre-recorded lectures onto the institute's Learning Management System (LMS) or delivering them via email. As a result, the emphasis was primarily placed on non-verbal learning, with an emphasis on writing, reading, and listening skills. Unfortunately, the development of speaking skills was often overlooked. While grammar, for instance, could be taught online through the provision of theory, exercises, and written practice, this approach primarily focused on rote memorisation of rules. These observations are further supported by the research conducted by Schaffner and Stefanutti (2022) and Öztürk-Karatas and Tunce (2020). Their findings indicated that 52% of respondents stated that speaking skills are better taught in face-to-face classes, and accordingly 64% of pre-service English teachers expressed that asynchronous online English courses are not conducive to effective speaking practice. The value of communicative grammar instruction lies in the fact that the act of speaking a language assists learners in transferring their understanding of grammar from the recesses of their minds to the forefront, or from 'slow memory' to 'quick memory' (EF English live, n.d., para.4). It is crucial for pre-service English language instructors to possess fluent and precise speaking skills in the language and for the context they intend to teach. This proficiency encompasses both accurate pronunciation and grammatical structure.

The COVID-19 pandemic showed within the first few weeks that neither instructors nor students were prepared for the sudden change to online teaching. At the same time, instructors realised that teaching is not just a one-way delivery of information through an LMS, but that it involves much more, such as the interaction between the information delivered and the students, and between the instructor and the students. We can speak of two types of learners: those who thrive on working alone, knowing that they can access the information, complete the tasks and exercises at their own pace, and stay focused throughout the course, and those who prefer to work as part of a learning community and enjoy knowing that they are not alone in their journey. The second type may find it difficult to stay motivated throughout the course without opportunities to interact with their peers and instructor.

Hodges et al. (2020) together with Gacs et al. (2020) argue that the shift to online teaching in HE institutions in March 2020 was not a fully developed transition, lacking the necessary pedagogical considerations and preparations for teaching languages online. The move to online learning simply extended what would have been covered in traditional classroom settings in the absence of a pandemic (Schaffner & Stefanutti, 2022). In numerous HE institutions, the shift to online learning has presented an opportunity for the advancement of flexible learning methodologies (Divjak et al., 2022). Consequently, many institutions have explored the implementation of the flipped classroom instructional approach. However, it is crucial to recognise that the availability and utilisation of technology infrastructure on campus, as well as the prevalence of online instruction, also influenced program readiness. This led to certain institutions having to delay learning and teaching activities due to insufficient information technology infrastructure for educators (Schaffner & Stefanutti, 2022; Crawford et al. (2020)). It was not enough for universities to possess robust information technology infrastructure; it was equally important to ensure that data protection was safeguarded by the platforms and applications used for online teaching. In Germany, universities have been deliberating on the varying levels of privacy protection provided by different web-conferencing platforms (Kissau et al., 2022). Moreover, the introduction of novel pedagogical approaches to online teaching, which may be unfamiliar to instructors, must be acknowledged. In Germany, for example, a number of universities had enlisted the expertise of e-learning specialists to conduct online teaching workshops for faculty members, along with monthly online teaching forums for sharing strategies (Kissau et al., 2022).

Like countless universities around the world, the Karlsruhe University of Education had to implement emergency remote teaching and learning (ERTL), also known as emergency remote education (ERE), and immediately change the delivery mode of its courses from face-to-face to fully remote. ERTL was a temporary shift in the delivery of education to an alternative delivery mode due to crisis circumstances. This includes using fully remote solutions for teaching and learning that would otherwise be delivered in-person, blended or hybrid. Unlike normal distance education, ERTL's primary goal was not to recreate a robust educational ecosystem, but to provide temporary access to education and educational support in a way that is quickly established and reliably available during emergencies or crises (Hodges et al., 2020). The university's English department's seminars delivered the use of fully remote teaching and learning solutions. However, as the semester progressed, it became apparent that students were not participating in group work as they should, preferring to work individually rather than interacting with their peers (whom they had never met before). They were unmotivated to follow the content and stated that they felt alone very often. We strongly believe that peer-to-peer interaction, as well as instructor-student interaction and group work, can enhance and complement student learning and even lead to better learning outcomes. It was therefore decided that in the post-COVID era, the seminar would move from a fully remote delivery to a remote synchronous delivery (RSD), where the seminar would be delivered using the flipped classroom (see part 2 of the Background section).

The research question that this study attempts to answer is: Can the combination of DLPs and the flipped classroom help pre-service English teachers improve their grammar and meet their communication and social needs in the post-pandemic era?

This book chapter consists of two main parts. The first part presents the context and the theoretical background, whereas the second part describes the material, sample, process, and method, as well as the study results and their discussion. The article concludes by summarising the findings and suggesting ideas for future research.

Remote Synchronous Delivery (RSD)

RSD is a model of remote teaching that has been used to move from face-to-face teaching to live online sessions, particularly after the outbreak of the COVID-19 pandemic (Cicha et al., 2021) when online teaching sessions became the new classroom reality. RSD takes the form of a series of pre-arranged webinars. Its main aim is to provide students with the least possible disruption to the learning process, so it is a good way to quickly change the way a class is run and mimic the face-to-face classroom experience (same class length, date, and time, and attendance requirements) on a videoconferencing platform. Such an approach needs to include the adaptation of the pedagogy that accompanies the class, such as the structure of the lecture format, physical activities, interactions, and considering the possibilities and limitations of online teaching and learning (Henriksen et al., 2020).

Flipped Classroom

We decided to deliver our online course on a flipped classroom basis, which is a blended learning model (a combination of synchronous and asynchronous teaching and learning sessions). It is a didactic concept that makes learning content available in a prepared form before the classroom event. The reason for choosing the flipped classroom approach is that we wanted to use the time together in the online 'classroom' for practice and application. The flipped classroom aims to create more space for interactive collaboration with learners and to shift traditional frontal teaching to self-learning (Kim et al., 2014). In a flipped classroom environment, students start the course by learning concepts and skills asynchronously. Learning can occur in a variety of ways, including watching videos, reading, doing interactive online activities, and taking quizzes. All work is completed prior to the synchronous component of the course. The synchronous component involves learning with tutors and peers and provides an opportunity for students to come together and explore complex tasks, solve problems, and build knowledge. The key to supporting learner motivation in online or blended learning environments is interactivity, which in this context refers to the ability of learners to be socially and cognitively engaged in interacting with content through learning materials, interacting with peers, and interacting with instructors (Anderson, 2003). In accordance with this classification, collaborative formats such as discussion, feedback, and small group work have a higher potential to support students' social interactions and engagement.

Digital Learning Paths (DLPs)

A DLP is an internet-based learning path (LP) that provides a series of coordinated tasks through interactive materials which can help learners develop the habit of independent and self-directed learning while working towards a specific learning goal. Besides visual formats, audio-visual formats can also be used to support learning (Windler & Wolf, 2021). DLPs can be a support tool for learners both in the classroom and at home as long as they are embedded in a meaningful way. DLPs can include Word, Excel, and PowerPoint documents, images, websites, links, notes, and activities like surveys, tests, quizzes, assignments, and debates. DLPs can also be implemented completely in the form of the flipped classroom concept, but learning phases can also alternate between digital media and traditional teaching methods (Roth & Wiesner, 2014). With transparent goals and expectations (Roth 2015), students can plan and organise their learning in time, process, and effort (Konrad & Traub, 2009). In addition to self-organised and independent practice and learning, an LP may ensure transparency of learning and performance expectations and provide differentiated support to students (Hessisches Schulportal, 2016). There are several ways in which DLPs can be used in the classroom. They can be used to introduce a new topic, for independent work or open-ended learning, to check learning objectives or exit from a topic, or they can simply be made available to students as an optional extra (Schmidt, 2009).

DLPs can be seen in these forms:

- Linear or expository arrangements, in which the learning content is presented in a prescribed, sequential order and in which students have relatively little choice about how they proceed.
- Branched or exploratory arrangements, where the emphasis is on the learner and their individual learning needs. Content can usually be explored via hypertext rather than sequentially by the learner.
- Complex arrangements where, depending on the learning scenario (usually problem-oriented and cooperative), the focus is on developing complex skills and

reaching the meta-level, reflecting the group's individual learning processes.

Methods, Materials, and Process

Research method

A mixed methods research design was conducted for this study. The purpose of choosing this type of research design was to arrive at a more robust conclusion, to address the weaknesses of one method through the use of the other, and to make it easier to generalise findings compared to the use of only qualitative research designs. Specifically, the study was based on the convergent parallel mixed methods research type, as our aim was to collect both quantitative and qualitative data at the same time and to analyse them separately.

Data was collected through an online post-grammar test and an online course evaluation survey consisting of 26 closed and open-ended questions about the content and overall delivery of the seminar. The content analysis method was employed to analyse the qualitative textual data. This methodology was especially effective in identifying and comprehending the themes, patterns, and associations existent in students' answers. Furthermore, it was helpful for exploring the extent to which the data can inform the theoretical claims present in research studies and contributed towards the quantification of the qualitative data.

Sample

The sample consisted of 29 pre-service teachers of English for secondary school who were on their master's course at the Karlsruhe

University of Education during the summer semester of 2022 and the winter semester of 2022–23. Specifically, there were 5 men and 24 women between the ages of 21 and 30.

Grammar test

An online grammar placement test was used pre- and post-seminar, containing 60 multiple-choice exercises to determine the pre-service teachers' level of grammar. With the help of this placement test, pre-service teachers would be placed in a level between A1 and C2 of the Common European Framework for Languages. The most frequent grammar mistakes made during this pre-grammar test determined the grammar topics taught during the seminar as well as the topic of the DLPs that the pre-service teachers constructed at the end of the seminar.

DLPs

The DLPs used for teaching grammar to pre-service teachers were structured according to the learning stages of Bloom's Taxonomy (knowledge, comprehension, application, and analysis or synthesis or evaluation) and were created in the university's LMS 'Innovation Space'. Our DLPs included interactive grammar exercises such as true or false, fill in the gaps, matching exercises, etc. Based on an automated scoring system, the pre-service teachers would only be able to access the grammar exercises according to the level (basic, intermediate, advanced) in which they were placed based on the points they had accumulated so far from the previous exercises. This tiered structure of exercises was complemented by the formative feedback function, which allowed students to check their answers and receive feedback at any time. In addition, our

DLPs tried to present grammar theory in a multimodal way, such as pictures, videos, and audio files, and placed the grammar in a digital storytelling framework, sometimes with a pedagogical agent, in the hope of increasing the attractiveness of DLPs.

Seminar

The seminar "Media Didactic Competence: LPs and Digital Storytelling for Grammar Teaching", in which these DLPs are produced, is part of the InDiKo project "Sustainable Integration of Digital Teaching and Learning Concepts", which started in May 2020 at the Karlsruhe University of Education (InDiKo, 2020–2023). The university's English department is also involved in the project and focuses its research on developing the media-didactic competencies of pre-service English teachers, while at the same time measuring their grammatical competence development, hence the creation of this seminar.

The synchronous phase of our seminar took the form of a weekly webinar that took place on the same day and time. The university decided to use the open-source web conferencing system BigBlueButton to replicate face-to-face teaching, and so did the English department. During the live sessions, the instructor used a grammar-based DLP (that was focused on a specific grammar topic and structured according to Bloom's Taxonomy) and taught his/her lesson by guiding the students through the DLP, which usually included group tasks, polls, brainstorming sessions, role-playing exercises, videos, pictures, quizzes, debates, etc., as they would be done in the classroom. The instructor was there to discuss the previous and new material and answer questions. During the exercises, students could use timed virtual breakout sessions to discuss and then return to share their ideas and conclusions. The final phase of the DLP would usually be for students to argue about the use of one grammar tense over another, to evaluate another grammar-focused DLP in terms of didactics and instructional design, or to start synthesising their own concepts for creating their own grammar-focused DLP in pairs (which they would also implement as a DLP on Innovation Space by the end of the seminar).

The asynchronous phase (courseware) of the seminar was in Stud IP, the virtual learning environment already in use at the university. It contained DLPs focused on technological pedagogical content knowledge theory, which included theory, quizzes, exercises, discussion areas, and additional readings to enrich students' knowledge and prepare them for the upcoming webinar. In addition to sending emails, the communication channel between students and between students and the instructor was always part of the DLPs to ensure a constant connection. Students could use this forum to ask their instructor questions and post and discuss answers with their peers depending on the requirements of the assignment. Another very important part of the DLPs found in the courseware is the reflection area, where the pre-service teachers were asked to reflect on the grammar focused DLP they engaged with during the webinar in terms of media didactics.

Results and Discussion

This study was conducted to investigate whether combining DLPs with flipped classroom can help pre-service teachers improve their grammatical knowledge while meeting their communicative and social needs in the post-COVID era. The results will be separated between grammatical knowledge and communicative and social needs.

Grammatical knowledge

The results of the online post-grammar test showed that 28 pre-service teachers (95,6%) improved their knowledge of English grammar during the seminar and scored much better than in the online pre-grammar test (moving from the 60% range to the 70% range), while one pre-service teacher (3,4%) scored the highest in the class (in the 80% range).

Communication and social needs

The online course evaluation survey revealed that 87% of students stated that they had profited largely from the way our seminar was conducted. The remaining 13% said that they were satisfied with the way the seminar was delivered but would not mind if it had been delivered completely asynchronously like the other seminars. By analysing the students' responses, 3 themes were identified: Dialogic learning, organised learning as well as interpersonal and community learning. Here are the most representative answers used by the pre-service English teachers when filling in the survey:

For organised learning:

"The fact that all instructions, materials, and assignments were included in a single DLP made my learning more organised."

"To me, DLPs are a pleasant way to go through the learning unit smoothly."

Organised learning is defined as "planned in a pattern or sequence with explicit or implicit aims. It involves a providing agency (person(s) or body) that facilitates the learning environment, and a method of instruction through which communication is organised. Instruction typically involves a teacher or a trainer who is engaged in communicating and guiding knowledge and skills with a view to bringing about learning" (Eurostat, 2016, p.15). DLPS can be employed as a means of providing a comprehensive repository for learning materials, encompassing (additional) theoretical content, (supplementary) exercises, and communication forums. This approach facilitates the integration of individual and group or pair learning, as well as student-lecturer communication, within a single digital platform, enhancing the efficiency of the learning process. The instructor has structured the DLP in a systematic manner, aligning the content and learning objectives with the knowledge to be transmitted.

For dialogic learning:

"Being shy, I often feel hesitant to share what I think with many people. The small breakout rooms and discussion forums were very important for me to have."

Dialogic Learning encompasses "a range of discourses concerned with the learning that happens within and through dialogue" (Davis & Francis, 2024, para. 1). The utilisation of online synchronous breakout rooms affords students the opportunity to engage in discourse within smaller groups, particularly those who may be more reserved. This setting allows them to express their opinions freely, with the understanding that their contributions will be confined to the in-group and not disseminated beyond. Additionally, as shy students may be reticent to express their opinions in class, this setting provides them with a space to do so, encouraging them to become more active participants in the learning process.

For interpersonal and community learning:

"The synchronous environment allows for a more fluid personal interaction and makes you feel like you are sitting in the classroom with your peers."

"The combination of synchronous and asynchronous learning environments was very important. It helped us to feel much more like a community working together towards the same goal. Being able to exchange ideas and opinions while seeing each other online made the learning environment so much better because you could put a face to a name."

"Compared to other seminars which are still delivered entirely at a distance, the opportunity to work with others in a synchronous meeting in pairs or groups reduced the feeling of loneliness on my student journey and increased the feeling of being connected with my fellow students.

"I liked that every DLP has a forum, where we can post questions that we may have at any time even after the class. Starting discussions with my peers and our lecturer can be very stimulating for my learning."

"With the live webinars and the communication forum, I never felt absent from lessons. It felt like I was in a virtual class, and I had everyone around me. It was like being in class but at home."

"It was as if we were going to school, but we were home. At first, I was worried about doing an online course and thought it would be different from a classroom course. To my surprise, I found that we quickly developed a sense of community and excitement that made learning enjoyable."

Interpersonal learning and community-based learning are in favour of the students who thrive in working through issues, ideas, and problems within a group [the social (interpersonal) learning style, n.d.]. In our context, students in the online synchronous classroom were intrinsically encouraged to participate in joint discussions and activities that facilitate the improvement of their skills and knowledge (Community-based learning, 2014). This approach benefits the entire community, with the goal of enhancing their English grammar knowledge, in our case.

With regard to previous studies, the findings of this study correspond with those reported by Salman et al. (2021). Their study was conducted with the aim of exploring student and teacher preparedness, delivery approaches, student engagement and activities, and evaluation and assessment in an RSD environment. Their findings confirmed that in "collaborative assignments, students felt a stronger connection with their partner through the RSD process versus in class as students had to schedule regular Zoom meetings to connect daily" (Salman et al., 2021, p. 287). They also reported that despite being taught in an RSD environment, there were still students who reported feeling lonely at times. This is not reflected in the results of the current study. However, it is understandable that for some students RSD cannot completely replace face-to-face teaching, as being on campus is also a sign that they need to start concentrating and preparing for their upcoming classes, something that some students might miss if they are only taught at home. Breakout rooms possess the capability to enhance motivation, efficiency, foster student connections, and instill the self-assurance required for active participation in meaningful discussions (Cadieux et al., 2020; Saltz & Heckman, 2020). According to the research conducted by Douglas (2023), it was discovered that students exhibit a higher tendency to express their thoughts and provide explanations when engaged in breakout room activities. Specifically, the study revealed that 20% of the participants stated they would consistently share their ideas, while 47% mentioned they would frequently do so. Additionally, 26% of the respondents indicated they would occasionally share their thoughts, whereas only 4% mentioned they would rarely engage in such discussions (Douglas, 2023).

In their study examining the lessons learned from the RSD model and its impact on students, teachers, and administrators, Antohi-Kominek and Salman (2021) also confirm that "students who are engaged participate in the class activities and perform equally well as in a face-to-face equivalent course. Those students who have previously experienced asynchronous online courses have commented that they wished online courses would be more like RSD courses" (p. 244). This combination of synchronous and asynchronous learning encourages students to interact with the materials and activities on the LMS platform, both with the instructor and with their peers (Tobing & Pranowo, 2020). In an RSD environment, instructors can use a variety of strategies to replicate onsite teaching and learning situations. For example, weekly discussion questions and forum posts on topics related to the course, role-playing exercises, debates, brainstorming sessions, think-pair-share, team-based case study discussions, problem-based learning exercises, as well as online breakout rooms during synchronous sessions can create valuable and engaging classroom learning experiences and ultimately help to foster a sense of collaboration and teamwork as students would experience in an on-campus classroom setting (Singh et al., 2021).

Conclusion

This study was designed to investigate whether DLPs combined with flipped classroom could help pre-service English language teachers develop their grammatical knowledge and meet their communication and social needs in the post-COVID era. It found that in the new reality of online teaching and learning, the combination of DLPs and flipped classroom with the help of synchronous webinars can prove to be an effective combination of approaches to support the teaching of English grammar to pre-service English teachers, while also contributing to the satisfaction of their communication and social needs. Taken together, these findings suggest that the use of DLPs and webinars can provide a more organised type of teaching compared to face-to-face teaching, whereas the small, timed breakout rooms, as well as the discussion and reflection areas, can be ideal and have a positive effect on shy students who are reluctant to share their thoughts in face-to-face classes, thus increasing individual engagement.

However, the use of digital media is not in itself conducive to learning. It does not directly suggest a better way of learning, nor does it automatically address students' need to be part of a community and to interact with their peers. It depends on the didactic embedding. Therefore, changing a course's mode of delivery does not only mean changing the format of the learning material, but more importantly, it means changing the pedagogy that accompanies the new course, in terms of how the learning material can best be communicated (knowledge) and how students interact with each other and with the instructor to process this material (social interaction).

Future research could focus on better understanding the learning, teaching, and social factors involved in planning and delivering DLP and webinar-based classes. Specifically, future research could explore the various pedagogical approaches that can complement this innovative combination, aiming to enhance both communicative practices and further develop tailored course design theories for instructing pre-service English teachers in English grammar in the post-COVID era.

Acknowledgments

This project is part of the "Qualitätsoffensive Lehrerbildung", a joint initiative of the Federal Government and the Länder, which aims to improve the quality of teacher training. The programme is funded by the Federal Ministry of Education and Research. The authors are responsible for the content of this publication.

Appendix

DLP no. 12

Guest key: Group12

References

Anderson, T. (2003). Modes of interaction in distance education: recent developments and research question. In M. G. Moore & T. Anderson (Eds.), *Handbook of Distance Education* (pp.129–144). Lawrence Erlbaum Associates.

Antohi-Kominek, A., & Salman, M. (2021). Remote Synchronous Delivery (RSD): Lessons learned from teaching during COVID-19. In I. Fayed & J. Cummings, (Eds.), *Teaching in the post-COVID-19 Era: World education dilemmas, teaching innovations and solutions in the age of crisis* (pp. 237–246). Retrieved from: https://link.springer.com/book/10.1007/978-3-030-74088-7

Cadieux, M., Campos-Zamora, M., Zagury-Orly, I., & Dzara, K. (2020). Journal club using virtual breakout rooms: interactive continuing education with no learner preparation during COVID-19. *Journal of Continuing Education in the Health Professions, 40*(4), 217–219. Retrieved from: https://journals.lww.com/jcehp/Fulltext/2021/04110/Journal_Club_Using_Virtual_Breakout_Rooms_.16.aspx

Cicha, K., Rizun, M., Rutecka, P., & Strzelecki, A. (2021). COVID-19 and higher education: first-year students' expectations toward distance learning. *Sustainability, 13*(1889). DOI: https://doi.org/10.3390/su13041889

Crawford, J. A., Butler-Henderson, K. A., Jurgen, R., & Malkawi, B. H. (2020). COVID-19: 20 countries' higher education intra-period digital pedagogy responses. *Journal of Applied Learning Teaching, 3*(1), 9–28. Retrieved from: https://journals.sfu.ca/jalt/index.php/jalt/article/view/191

Davis, B., & Francis, K. (2024). *Dialogic Learning. Discourses on Learning in Education.* Retrieved from: https://learningdiscourses.com/discourse/dialogic-learning/

Divjak, B., Rienties, B., Iniesto, F., Vondra, P., & Zizak, M. (2022). Flipped Classrooms in higher education during the Covid-19 pandemic: findings and future research reccomendations. *International Journal of Educational Technology in Higher*

Education, 19(9), 1–24. Retrieved from: https://educational technologyjournal.springeropen.com/articles/10.1186/s41239-021-00316-4

Douglas, S. (2023). Achieving online dialogic learning using break-out rooms. *Research in Learning Technology, 31*. Retrieved from: https://journal.alt.ac.uk/index.php/rlt/article/view/2882

European University Association. (2020). European Higher Education in the Covid-19 crisis. Brussels: European University Association. Retrieved from: https://eua.eu/downloads/publications/briefing_european%20higher%20education%20in%20the%20covid-19%20crisis.pdf

Eurostat. (2016). Classification of learning activities (CLA) Manual. Luxemburg: Publications Office of the European Union. Retrieved from https://ec.europa.eu/eurostat/documents/3859598/7659750/KS-GQ-15-011-EN-N.pdf

Gacs, A., Goertler, S., & Spasova, S. (2020). Planned online language education versus crisis prompted online language teaching: Lessons for the future. *Foreign Language Annals, 53*(2), 380–392. Retrieved from: https://onlinelibrary.wiley.com/doi/abs/10.1111/flan.12460

Henriksen, D., Creely, E., & Henderson, M. (2020). Folk Pedagogies for Teacher Educator Transitions: Approaches to Synchronous Online Learning in the Wake of COVID-19. *Journal of Technology and Teacher Education. 28*. 201–209. Retrieved from: (PDF) Folk Pedagogies for Teacher Educator Transitions: Approaches to Synchronous Online Learning in the Wake of COVID-19 (researchgate.net).

Hodges, C., Moore, S., Lockee, B., Trust, T., & Bond, A. (2020, March 27). *The difference between emergency remote teaching and online learning*. EDUCASE. Retrieved June 29, 2023, from The Difference Between Emergency Remote Teaching and Online Learning | EDUCAUSE Review.

Kim, M. K., Kim, S. M., Khera, O., & Getman, J. (2014). The experience of three flipped classrooms in an urban university: an exploration of design principles. *The Internet and Higher Education, 22*. 37–50. Retrieved from: https://www.science

direct.com/science/article/abs/pii/S1096751614000219 https://www.sciencedirect.com/science/article/abs/pii/S1096751614000219

Kissau, S., Davin, K., Brunsmeier, S., & Herazo, J. S. (2022). Language Teacher Preparation in a pandemic: An International Comparison of Responses to Covid-19. *NECTFL Review, 88*, 17–35. Retrieved from: https://eric.ed.gov/?id=EJ1339811

Konrad, K., & Traub, S. (2009). *Selbstgesteuertes Lernen*. Schneider.

Öztürk Karataş T., & Tuncer, H. (2020). Sustaining Language Skills Development of Pre-Service EFL Teachers despite the COVID-19 Interruption: A Case of Emergency Distance Education. *Sustainability, 12*(19). Retrieved from: https://www.mdpi.com/2071-1050/12/19/8188

Roth, J., & Wiesner, H. (2014). Lernpfade – Ein Weg zur selbstständigen und sinnvollen Nutzung von digitalen Werkzeugen durch Schüler/innen. In Roth, J. & Armes, J. (Eds.), *Beiträge zum Mathematikunterricht* (pp.1003–1006). WTM-Verlag. Retrieved from: https://www.juergen-roth.de/veroeffentlichungen/2014/roth_wiesner_lernpfade.pdf

Roth, J. (2015). Lernpfade – Definition, Gestaltungskriterien und Unterrichtseinsatz. In J. Roth, E. Süss-Stepancik, & H. Wiesner, (Hrg.), *Medienvielfalt im Mathematikunterricht. Lernpfade als Weg zum Ziel* (pp. 3–26). Springer.

Salman, M., Fobler-Cressy, P., Habib, R., Elkady, D., & Mohammed, G. (2021). Remote synchronous delivery for Interior Design Education: The shift towards innovative paradigms in design teaching approaches. In I. Fayed & J. Cummings, (Eds.), *Teaching in the post-COVID-19 Era: World education dilemmas, teaching innovations and solutions in the age of crisis* (pp. 281–290). Retrieved from: https://link.springer.com/book/10.1007/978-3-030-74088-7

Saltz, J. & Heckman, R. (2020). Using structured pair activities in a distributed online breakout room. *Online Learning, 24*(1), 227–244. Retrieved from: https://olj.onlinelearningconsortium.org/index.php/olj/article/view/1632

Schaffner, S., & Stefanutti, I. (2022). The impact of the Covid-19 Pandemic on Language Teaching in Higher Education, CercleS survey. *Verbum, 13*. Retrieved from: https://www.redalyc.org/journal/6947/694773777007/694773777007.pdf

Schmidt, R. (2009). *Selbstgesteuertes Lernen durch Lernpfade* [Paper Präsentation]. 100. MNU-Kongress, Regensburg, Germany. Retrieved from: selbstgesteuertes-lernen-durch-lernpfade-RpmQy6E0Ro.pdf

Singh, J., Steele, K., & Singh, L. (2021). Combining the best of online and face-to-face learning: Hybrid and blended learning approach for Covid-19, post-vaccine, & post-pandemic world. *Journal of Educational Technology, 50*(2), 140–171. Retrieved from: https://journals.sagepub.com/doi/10.1177/00472395211047865

Tobing, R. L., & Pranowo, D. D. (2020). Blended learning in French intermediate grammar learning: Is it effective? *Journal of Education Horizon, 39*(3), 645–654. Retrieved from: https://journal.uny.ac.id/index.php/cp/article/view/32035

Windler, M., & Wolf, K. (2021). *Entwicklung und Erprobung digitaler Lernpfade für den Mathematikunterricht in heterogenen Klassen*. http://dx.doi.org/10.17877/DE290R-22338

Webpages

Community-based learning. (2014, March 3). The Glossary of Education Reform. https://www.edglossary.org/community-based-learning/

Five reasons why speaking English is a great way to learn it. (n.d.). EF English live. https://englishlive.ef.com/en/blog/study-tips/five-reasons-speaking-english-great-way-learn/

Hessisches Schulportal (2016). *Online-Lernpfade leichtgemacht*. https://dms-portal.bildung.hessen.de/elc/fortbildung/web_u/lernpfad/infowizard-lernpfad/index.html

Pädagogische Hochschule Karlsruhe (01.05.2020–31.12.2023). *Sustainable integration of subject didactic digital teaching-*

learning concepts (InDiKo). https://www.ph-karlsruhe.de/projekte/indiko

The social (interpersonal) learning style. (n.d.). Learning-styles-online.com. https://www.learning-styles-online.com/style/social-interpersonal/

Integrating Critical Discourse Analysis in the Language Classroom: A Proposed Framework for Developing Media Critical Literacy

Dia Evagorou-Vassiliou
King's College London, England
diaevagorou@gmail.com

Abstract

The COVID-19 pandemic has brought about significant challenges that have highlighted the importance of media literacy, especially in navigating the surge of misinformation. This paper addresses the necessity of integrating Critical Language Awareness (CLA) into language education to enhance students' ability to critically evaluate media

---

How to cite this book chapter:
Evagorou-Vassiliou, D. 2024. Integrating Critical Discourse Analysis in the Language Classroom: A Proposed Framework for Developing Media Critical Literacy. In: Athanasiou, A., Hadjiconstantinou, S. and Christoforou, M. (Eds.) *Innovative Language Teaching Practices in Higher Education in a Post-COVID Era*. Pp. 97–122. London: Ubiquity Press. DOI: https://doi.org/10.5334/bdd.f. License: CC BY 4.0

discourse. Drawing on Critical Discourse Analysis (CDA) and Systemic Functional Grammar (SFG), the proposed framework equips higher education undergraduate students with the skills to analyze media texts critically. This approach not only improves language proficiency but also fosters critical engagement with socio-political contexts, ultimately promoting responsible information consumption. The framework includes practical implementation steps, encompassing both online and face-to-face activities, enabling students to understand how language shapes social realities. Emphasizing a hybrid educational model that blends technology with critical pedagogy, the study addresses the evolving demands of the post-pandemic digital landscape.

Introduction

The COVID-19 pandemic has unleashed unprecedented challenges, particularly manifesting a profound impact on global digital systems (Lathouris, 2021); its ramifications transcend immediate contexts and resonate with future crises. This "infodemic" (World Health Organization, 2020) has exacerbated the dissemination of fake news and conspiracy narratives, fostering confusion and eroding public trust. These developments have posed significant hindrances to public communication, democratic processes, and mental health. As digital media became the primary source of information, the necessity for enhanced media literacy became evident, particularly for young people navigating this complex landscape. Amidst the struggle to discern reliable information from misinformation, individuals have faced a pressing need for heightened vigilance in evaluating digital sources. Hence, the necessity of equipping individuals with essential skills for adeptly navigating digital communication (Buckingham, 2020) became evident.

In the post-COVID era, marked by the ubiquity of media and the rampant spread of misinformation, the demand for comprehensive media literacy education is more crucial than ever. The rapid adoption of digital technologies necessitates an educational shift towards hybrid learning models that integrate technology with critical pedagogy. Language learning, therefore, must also adapt to these challenges, employing methodologies that prioritize digital literacy and interactive engagement. Technological advancements are considered essential for enriching online interactive learning experiences and facilitating remote language acquisition (Stockwell, 2021).

This paper proposes a framework to address these educational challenges by promoting critical literacy through the enhancement of Critical Language Awareness (CLA) and effective use of technology. CLA is essential for developing the cognitive and analytical skills needed to resist manipulation and counteract misinformation. By encouraging a critical approach to media and communication, CLA enables individuals to identify biased language and persuasive techniques in texts, fostering an ability to distinguish between factual information and deceptive content (Svalberg, 2021). Moreover, emphasizing the importance of contextualizing discourse within socio-political and cultural contexts, CLA aids in identifying potential sources of misinformation and fosters critical engagement with language, instilling a habit of skepticism and inquiry. Integrating CLA into educational curricula (Wallace, 1992) emerges as a crucial step toward promoting responsible information consumption by empowering individuals to evaluate information critically, verify claims, and consider multiple perspectives, thereby acting as a deterrent against the spread and acceptance of misinformation.

For enhancing learners' CLA and critical media literacy in university language learners, the framework proposed draws on Critical Discourse Analysis (CDA), the social constructionist perspective of learning (Lave & Wenger, 2020), and the Communicative Language Teaching (CLT) approach (Savignon, 1987); it amalgamates conventional teaching methods with technology-driven activities to nurture indispensable soft skills vital for active engagement in media discourse.

Language Centers play a crucial role in advancing CLA and media critical literacy. They can therefore implement the proposed framework, and integrate CDA into their methodologies, enhancing students' language proficiency and critical skills necessary for effective media discourse navigation. Their diverse roles include designing curricula, providing training for language instructors, offering resources and pedagogical support, and fostering media critical literacy within the community.

Literature Review and Theoretical Framework

To enhance students' critical thinking capabilities and empower them to engage meaningfully with language and media, the integration of CLA through CDA emerges as a promising approach (Fairclough, 2015; Buckingham, 2020).

Grounded in Critical Linguistics, CDA offers a robust framework for scrutinizing language usage in social contexts, unveiling power dynamics, and examining how media discourse perpetuates societal norms (Fairclough, 1992a). It enables learners to approach media and political discourse with a discerning eye, fostering a nuanced comprehension of social issues and ideologies.

At its core, CDA delves into the intricate interplay between language, societal structures, power dynamics, and ideologies within both immediate and broader societal contexts. Central to CDA is the notion of 'representation,' encompassing the discursive techniques used to construct, categorize, and assess subjects and objects while simultaneously exerting symbolic power through language or other semiotic practices (Fairclough, 1992 p. 57). Discourse within this framework is shaped by social conditions and constructs social and cultural realities. Through exploring how language molds social reality, CDA enables students to cultivate a deeper understanding of the intricacies inherent in communication and discourse.

The approach outlined in this study suggests using the Systemic Functional Grammar (SFG) model of meanings (Halliday, 1994) to analyze media discourse and examine subjectivity and ideological positioning. In particular, the transitivity (Halliday & Matthiessen, 2004) and appraisal (Martin & White, 2005) tools are employed to explore the analytical categories of social actor representation and evaluative language. The former is proposed as a tool for ideological analysis to identify the representation of actors or processes. Social actors, defined as active participants in social practices (Van Leeuwen, 2008), possess considerable causal impact on events, and their portrayal in media texts can offer valuable insights into the discourses espoused, the media outlet's interpretation of a given phenomenon (Hardt-Mautner, 1995), and the strategies employed for legitimization or the attribution of responsibility and blame. The representation of social actors in media texts encompasses visibility, roles and functions, relationships, stereotyping, and emphasis. Van Dijk (2008) showed how ideologies are constructed, maintained, and reinforced through language and social practices by investigating the cognitive processes underlying discourse production of news actors. Fowler (1991) has focused on the representation of marginalized groups in the British press by applying SFG to identify socially significant patterns. Wodak (2015) showed how media texts were utilized by political elites to legitimize their actions, establish identities, and disseminate ideologies. Secondly, the investigation of evaluative language plays a vital role in unraveling subjectivity and ideological positioning within news discourse. It functions as a tool for interpreting the world, encompassing elements such as 'stance-taking and attitudinal positioning' (Bednarek, 2006 p. 21). Extending the concept of transitivity, the appraisal framework offers valuable insights into investigating evaluative meanings and the subjectivity of the authorial voice within news discourse. Appraisal encompasses language features navigating emotions, judgments, and valuations, enabling a comprehensive exploration of the evaluative dimension.

In this study, meanings are scrutinized across three strata: ideational, interpersonal, and textual, with a particular focus on the portrayal of social actors and evaluative language. According to Halliday (1994), these metafunctions play distinct roles in discourse analysis. The ideational and interpersonal metafunctions are especially relevant in this context, where they help decode underlying ideologies and attribute power or responsibility in news content. The ideational function examines verb phrases to spot types of semantic processes and active or passive roles assigned to participants. In contrast, the interpersonal metafunction addresses the subjective presence of the writer or speaker within texts, including their stances, evaluations, and their influence on readers (Thompson & Hunston, 2000).

Methodology

This section outlines the recommended framework for the initial integration of CDA into the classroom environment. The framework incorporates a blend of online and face-to-face activities, with facilitated access to authentic material such as news articles. The implementation of online collaborative learning practices, such as virtual group projects and discussions can enhance student participation and peer interaction in virtual language courses (Godwin-Jones, 2020). Hence student-led CDA analyses and collective discussions form integral components, allowing for the examination and interpretation of findings. Technology-enhanced activities, including revision quizzes, participatory learning activities, peer analysis, and collaborative interpretation of meanings, are incorporated into the framework. Instructors are provided with a set of critical questions (see Table 1) to guide them throughout the process.

Steps	Indicative Critical Questions and Deliverables
1 (in person) – Explain the significance of CDA in modern communication – Introduce CDA's basic principles, with a focus on the analytical categories of social actor representation and evaluative language	– What is the topic? Who is the author? Who is the audience? – What is the source of the information? Investigate the credibility and reputation of the source. Is it known for accuracy and reliability, or does it have a particular bias or agenda? – How is discourse structured? – What is the purpose of the text or media content? Consider the author's or producer's intentions. Are they informing, persuading, entertaining, or advocating for a particular viewpoint?

(Continued)

Steps	Indicative Critical Questions and Deliverables
	– What is the tone and language used? Pay attention to the tone of the text or media content. Is it objective and impartial, or does it exhibit emotional language, loaded terms, or sensationalism? – How are identities negotiated and how are ideologies constructed in discourse? – How do the lexicogrammar choices of the editor/speaker reinforce or challenge societal norms or reflect power, inequity, or stereotyping of people/groups? – Are there any logical fallacies or flawed reasoning? Look for inconsistencies, contradictions, or logical leaps in the argument presented. Are conclusions supported by valid reasoning and evidence? – How is language used to demonstrate ideology? – Who has the constructed power? Who is being dominated? – What perspectives are included or omitted? Evaluate whether the text or media content presents a balanced view by including multiple perspectives and voices. Are alternative viewpoints considered, or is there a one-sided presentation of information? – Are there any implicit biases or assumptions? Scrutinize the underlying assumptions and biases that may influence the content. Consider the cultural, political, or ideological perspectives that may shape the narrative.
2 (in person) – Explain and apply the SFG and appraisal model in texts – Provide guided analysis of media texts	– Who is the actor, and who is the goal of action/ victim? What is the process of action? When are active and passive constructions used? Are there any nominalisations, and how are they used? – What linguistic phenomena are observed in headlines?

(Continued)

Steps	Indicative Critical Questions and Deliverables
	– Is there use of evaluative or emotional language? – What is the positioning of the author (engagement) or the values expressed? – How is modality used to show the speaker's judgement? – Are words/phrases repeated throughout the text? Which ones and how often? – What is the societal and historical context of the text?
3 (online) – Follow up – revise theory through Moodle Quiz (types of multiple choice and short answer) on linguistic phenomena taught in class – Facilitate meta-analysis, and encourage students to share their reasoning	(Design questions that prompt critical thinking and allocate time for students to reflect on the quiz answers)
4 (in person / online in Zoom breakout rooms) – Divide students into small groups of 2–3 persons and assign them for analysis different news articles according to their interests	
5 (online through Zoom platform or Teams) – Brainstorm per group on the analysis of the text assigned	

(Continued)

Steps	Indicative Critical Questions and Deliverables
6 (in person) – Online presentations by student groups – Peer analysis	– Exemplification of their analysis per group – Sharing of observations and insights – Provision of students' collective comments to their colleagues regarding the critical analysis of their texts
7 (in person) Rewrite/reconstruct texts applying CDA to improve their content and structure	– How can I incorporate more inclusive / anti-oppressive language to the texts assigned? – How can I incite action through linguistic codes?
8 Evaluation	– Monitoring throughout and assessing students' progress in using CDA

Table 1: Proposed Instructor's Guide for Introducing CDA.

Exploring Agency and Responsibility: Social Actors and Their Semantic Roles

This section underscores the significance of exploring ideational meaning by closely examining how linguistic representations of agency shape the portrayal of key participants in various processes and events. Practical examples are provided to illustrate the analysis of agency through the lens of transitivity in authentic media texts. The concept of agency and its linguistic manifestations are pivotal in CDA and SFL, as they illuminate actors, power dynamics, responsibility, and accountability (Halliday & Matthiessen, 2004; Van Leeuwen, 2008). Different modes of representing agency can accentuate or diminish an action, highlight or obscure accountability, portray agents as culpable or innocent, and attribute blame or credit for their actions.

In scrutinizing the representation of agency and responsibility, the analysis facilitates identifying the process types where the actors participate within authentic articles. Table 2 presents the classification utilized for this purpose, and several illustrative examples are provided to identify processes and roles.

P=Process	Action/ Category of Meaning	Critical function	Participant role
P-BEVAVIORAL = behavioural	behavioral actions	identifying the behavior of actors	Behaver
P-MATERIAL = material	doing physical actions in the real world	attributing responsibility to actors	Actor Goal Beneficiary Range Agent
P-VERBAL = verbal	Saying	attributing responsibility to actors	Sayer Receiver Verbiage
P-MENTAL = mental	sensing (feeling, wanting, thinking, and perceiving)	identifying mental state/positioning of actors	Senser Phenomenon
P-EXISTENTIAL = existential	Exist		Existent
P-RELATIONAL = relational	being or becoming	identifying traits/ attributes of actors	Carrier Attribute Token Value
Circumstantial – adverbial elements		identifying contextual factors (circumstance, accompaniment, cause, location, manner, role, matter)	

Table 2: Process Types and Roles in SFG (Halliday, 1994).

Material processes entail deliberate physical actions that impact other entities, emphasizing the active role of the agent in causing the action and achieving the desired outcome. These processes typically involve an actor or agent initiating the activity and a goal being affected by them, highlighting the individual's capacity to exert authority, exercise agency, and interact with the world. The assignment of the role of Actor can uncover the representation of the assignment of power, blaming, responsibility, and victimization. Verbal processes, revolve around communicative activities, underscoring the individual's ability to articulate thoughts and intentions through language. When attributed the role of Sayer, analysis can spot traces of discourses circulated or challenged by the participant and possible discursive inconsistencies. Both material and verbal processes empower participants with a significant degree of agency, allowing them to assert their will and influence the world around them.

An (invented) example of news piece might state:

> Ex.1: "The government [**ACTOR**] implemented [**P-MATERIAL**] [strict lockdown measures **GOAL/ACTION**] to curb the spread of COVID-19."

This sentence attributes responsibility to the government, highlighting its active role in taking measures against the pandemic. The use of the material process "implemented" emphasizes the government's authority and decision-making power. The beneficiary implied is public health.

Below, an authentic excerpt (*Le Monde*, 06.03.2013):

> Ex.2: (translation) Admittedly, the austerity package imposed [**P-VERBAL**] by Angela Merkel [**SAYER**], in exchange for unprecedented solidarity with failed states, **has put** [**P-MATERIAL transitive**] **European growth** [**GOAL**] on the gr/ound.

In ex.2, material and verbal processes offer insights into Merkels' level of responsibility. In particular, the editor asserts that the Chancellor (Sayer) imposed austerity measures (verbal process), which adversely affected EU economic growth (goal of the process). Merkel is held accountable for hindering European growth (material process). The use of the adverb 'admittedly' serves to reinforce the attribution of responsibility. Upon examining the entire text, it became evident that Sayer's role was predominant. The author employed a distancing strategy by indirectly attributing statements and actions to Merkel, rather than using direct quotation. This approach creates a sense of detachment from Merkel's discourse and placed responsibility on the Chancellor for her words and actions.

Ex.3 (*The Times*, 30.03.2010) below shows how relational processes delineate characteristics and construct a comprehensive profile of an individual. The assignment of the role of Identifier enables to identify attributions, characteristics, analogies, and metaphorical representations. The excerpt below underscores Merkel's significant role during the EU summit relating the Greek crisis, as indicated by the use of relational processes:

> Ex.3: This week has confirmed that Angela Merkel **[IDENTIFIED]** is **[P-RELATIONAL]** the towering figure of European politics.

The category of mental processes encompasses the expression of cognitive operations and psychological states, including perception, cognitive processes, motivation, affective states, and evaluative decision-making. The following analysis delineates the shift in the positioning of the IMF due to political pressures:

Ex.4: It appears that **the IMF [SENSER] succumbed** [**P-MENTAL**] too easily to political pressures during both the boom and the bust.

(The Guardian, 18.05.2012)

Comparing Patterns of Transitivity in News Headlines

Below is a new story summary and examples of newspaper headlines about the aforementioned story.

News story: On May 25, 2020, George Floyd, a 46-year-old black man, was murdered in Minnesota by police officer Derek Chauvin. Floyd was detained for allegedly using counterfeit currency, and Chauvin restrained him for over nine minutes by kneeling on his neck. J. Alexander Kueng and Thomas Lane assisted Chauvin in restraining Floyd, with Lane also pointing a pistol at Floyd's head. fourth officer, Tou Thao, prevented bystanders from interfering.

> Ex. 5: **Chauvin: Jail for just 22yrs ...but out in 15: Cop who killed George Floyd is sentenced** [The Daily Mirror, UK, 26 June 2021]
>
> Ex.6: **Hundreds demand justice in Minneapolis after the police killing of George Floyd** [J., Minneapolis, The Guardian, 27 May 2020]
>
> Ex. 7: **George Floyd case: Protests erupt across the country after Minnesota man's death** [H. McKay, Fox News, 28 May 2020]
>
> Ex.8: **Joe Biden takes a firm stand against the police murder of George Floyd.** [Brown, S.M., Tennessee Tribune, 18 June, 2020]

The aforementioned narrative exhibits distinct variations in the portrayal of actors, reflecting different focal points. Headline

1 places emphasis on the accountable agent (i.e., policeman) involved in the act of killing (i.e., action process) of George Floyd (i.e., goal of action). Notably, the headline employs a derogatory tone through the inclusion of the adverb "just" and the phrase "but out in 15," intensifying the sense of culpability. In contrast, Headline 2 utilizes nominalization ("killing") to report the process of action, with the agent referenced within a circumstantial phrase. Headline 3 presents a vaguer account of the action, utilizing circumstantial phrases and nominalization, with the term "death" employed instead of more precise lexical choices such as "killing" or "murdering." Furthermore, the agent is vaguely identified as the "Minnesota man," omitting specific naming, and the sentence structure assumes an agentless passive voice. Of notable significance is the absence of any reference to police brutality in Headline 3, as the act of killing is situated within the framework of civil unrest, disorder, casualties, and the destruction resulting from the violent behavior of the demonstrators. In contrast, Headline 4 explicitly identifies the actor and employs a nominalization circumstantial prepositional phrase to describe the action. The term 'murder' is deliberately selected, indicating a negative evaluation of the action by the editor. Moreover, the voice of Biden assumes a firm stance against the action, implicitly reflecting the perspective of the editor. Comparatively, the transitivity patterns employed by the editors reveal their respective perspectives concerning the actor and its impact on the goal. Headlines 1, 2, and 4 assign culpability to police officers for the act of homicide, whereas headline 3 suggests a lack of accountability on the part of the police. Furthermore, the term "death" is characterized by vagueness within the context of civil unrest. The ideological orientation of Fox News is evident in its presentation, which tends to align with conservative perspectives.

Analysing Evaluative Language and Author's Positioning

To analyze the text's interpersonal meanings embedded within the language and better understand the speaker's orientation to discourse or the stance of actors mentioned, the instructor and students can apply the appraisal categories (Table 3).

Category	Description
Affect	– How participants and processes are assessed by reference to emotional responses/evaluation of things/processes/states, explicit/implicit statements of (dis)likes, (dis)approval, (dis)agreement, and other subjective responses. Directly relates to mood.
Judgement	– Moral evaluation of human behavior through words/phrases expressing positive or negative judgments/opinions/assessments. The categories of judgment—capacity/tenacity/ propriety—refer to the ability, determination, and appropriateness of actions or behavior.
Appreciation	– Positive or negative aesthetic or functional evaluation of things/processes/states of affairs.
Engagement	– The voice of the author/speaker, including monogloss (facts/author's interpretations/presuppositions), dialogic contraction (disclaim/proclaim), and dialogic expansion (entertain/attribute). It describes the level of commitment/involvement/alignment with the topic and involves expressing certainty/doubt/likelihood/duty.
Modality	– Language used to indicate the speaker's/writer's attitude towards the truth value of a statement, including modal verbs and adverbs expressing different degrees of possibility/necessity/certainty. Modality and engagement work together to convey evaluation and attitude.

(Continued)

Category	Description
Graduation	– Comprises force (intensity/quantity in terms of amount/time/space), enhancement/focus (sharpening/softening), and fulfillment (qualification of processes).

Table 3: Appraisal categories (Halliday & Matthiessen, 2004).

To illustrate the application of the appraisal categories above, here is an (invented) editorial example:

> Ex.9: "The [delayed response JUDGMENT: negative judgment of capability and propriety] by health authorities [exacerbated the crisis APPRECIATION: negative evaluation of the situation] causing [unnecessary suffering AFFECT: negative emotional response]."

The sentence above evaluates the actions of health authorities, attributing blame and emphasizing the negative consequences of their delayed response. The language used conveys strong disapproval and highlights the perceived failure in managing the crisis effectively.

Below, an appraisal analysis of a specific section from a leader article is presented.

Text 1: Armageddon [negative APPRECIATION, negative GRADUATION: force] **Ready**

> Eurozone authorities are preparing for a Greek exit after Sunday's elections. *But* [ENGAGEMENT:contract:disclaim:counter] concessions look more *likely* [ENGAGEMENT:expand:entertain:probability].
>
> The European Commission has denied that it is working on contingency plans for a Greek exit from the single currency. The Commission "is not a <u>disaster movie screenwriter</u>" [negative JUDGEMENT for

Commission:propriety], it *says* [ENGAGEMENT:attribution:acknowledgement].

This is implausible [negative JUDGEMENT for EC not working on contingency plans] or, *if true* [ENGAGEMENT:expand:entertain:probability], alarming [negative JUDGEMENT for EC]. There is a **real** [positive GRADUATION:FOCUS] chance that the result of Sunday's Greek elections could [ENGAGEMENT:expand:entertain:probability] precipitate the country's swift exit from the euro. In which case, there should be [ENGAGEMENT:expand:entertain:probability] contingency plans to limit the damage to the rest of the Eurozone financial system.

But it still *seems* [ENGAGEMENT:expand:entertain:probability] more *likely* [ENGAGEMENT:expand:entertain:probability] that immediate crisis will [Evidential modality:prediction, inferring from results/reasoning] be averted and that a way will be found for Greece to stagger on within the currency bloc, *even if* [ENGAGEMENT:contract disclaim:counter] this merely postpones its eventual departure. It may [ENGAGEMENT:expand:entertain:probability] be **less** [negative GRADUATION:FORCE:intensification:quality] **Apocalypse Now** [negative APPRECIATION for Grexit, negative GRADUATION: force: intensification: process/vigour] and **more** [positive GRADUATION:FORCE:intensification:quality] **The Day After Tomorrow** [negative APPRECIATION for Grexit, negative GRADUATION: force:intensification:process/vigour]. It is **highly** [GRADUATION:FORCE:intensification:degree] *likely* [ENGAGEMENT:expand:entertain:probability] that Sunday's poll will [Evidential modality:prediction, inferring from results/reasoning] be inconclusive [negative APPRECIATION for elections] as last month's elections, after which it proved [ENGAGEMENT:contract:proclaim:en dorse] *impossible* [ENGAGEMENT:disclaim] [negative APPRECIATION for Greek elections] for any combination of parties to form a government.

But opinion polls suggest that Syriza, the far-left [negative JUDGEMENT for Syriza: normality] grouping led by Alexis Tsipras, could do well [positive JUDGEMENT for Tsipras:capacity], **enough** to form a government and carry out its pledge to abandon the austerity measures agreed as part of Greece's bailout. Mr. Tsipras says that he is committed [positive JUDGEMENT for Tsipras:veracity] to keeping Greece in the Eurozone. Since a big [negative GRADUATION: quantification] majority of the Greek people want [positive AFFECT:desire] to stay in, he is **hardly** [negative GRADUATION:FORCE] going to say anything else [negative implicit JUDGEMENT for Tsipras:veracity]. But he is threatening to push Greece towards a disorderly exit [negative JUDGEMENT for Tsipras:propriety] as a way of putting pressure on Germany to loosen the terms of the bailout. [...]

The Eurozone Carry On could [ENGAGEMENT: expand: entertain: probability] run for a while yet [ENGAGEMENT:contract:disclaim:counter]. But [ENGAGEMENT:contract:disclaim:counter], after a long prevarication, things at the last *May* [ENGAGEMENT:expand:entertain:probability] well move **very** [pre-modification adverb GRADUATION:force degree up-scale for process] quickly [positive APPRECIATION:reaction] *indeed* [ENGAGEMENT:PROCLAIM:affirm:modals of expectation]. With Greece facing its six-straight year of recession, it gets ever more *likely* [ENGAGEMENT:expand:entertain:probability] that both sides will *eventually* [ENGAGEMENT:PROCLAIM:affirm:modal of expectation]: modals of expectation] opt for **Independence Day**.

(*The Times*, June 14, 2012)

The leader article above presents the Greek exit from the EU as a cosmological scenario, negatively appraised (category of appreciation), using strategic lexical choices ("Armageddon") to frame the situation with a sense of drama. The author encourages readers to associate the crisis with catastrophic events through cultural references and metaphorical language. This effect is further intensified (graduation: scale up) with semantic repetition and overlexicalization through synonyms of disaster scenarios ("Apocalypse Now", "The Day After Tomorrow", "Independence Day"), preparing the reader for the Grexit possibilities and its impact. The frequent use of engagement (category entertain, possibility) and modals foster hypothetical scenarios (e.g. epistemic stance adverbials such as "likely", modal adjectives such as "unclear"), modal auxiliaries with low possibility value ("should be," "seems," "it may," "appears," "could"), and nouns ("likelihood"). Greek's positive emotions towards staying in the euro are identified through affect, category desire.

The author (through engagement) disclaims the Grexit scenario, presenting an alternative (concessions) as a positive outcome (engagement: affirm and proclaim). Also, the negative judgements towards the EC, show negative appraisal and critique of the EC for not working on contingency plans. The author is also positioned towards Tsipras through negative judgements of veracity, capacity, and propriety. Official sources are quoted, but the author negatively evaluates their responses, suggesting a lack of action and poor management. Political leaders' statements are reported indirectly, creating distance and allowing for different perspectives. The reported speech is framed and interpreted by the writer, who withholds authority and legitimacy from the leaders' statements.

Discussion and Conclusions

Discussion

CLA and media literacy are crucial in today's digital landscape, especially post-pandemic, where misinformation has surged. In the contemporary post-pandemic context, students must develop soft skills such as analyzing, assessing, and effectively communicating information, which are essential for fostering critical reading and media literacy. Media literacy education plays a crucial role in evaluating media content, critically navigating the complexities of the digital media ecosystem, and mitigating the spread of misinformation.

A hybrid educational paradigm, combining technology with critical pedagogy, can address the evolving demands of the post-pandemic era. Information and Communication Technology (ICT) tools enhance interactive learning, allowing students to apply analytical categories and critical skills in a dynamic environment (Gillen & Barton, 2010).

The integration of CDA and SFG principles into language teaching curriculum has demonstrated significant benefits, beyond enhancing language proficiency, comprehension of language-related concepts, and communication sensitivity. CDA techniques are particularly valuable for English as a foreign language learners, aiding in the acquisition of linguistic competencies and critical analytical skills. By scrutinizing meanings across ideational, interpersonal, and textual strata, students gain a deeper understanding of how language shapes social realities and power dynamics in today's interconnected world. Integrating CDA into the curriculum cultivates critical awareness of sociopolitical dimensions in media texts, and critical thinking. Such a multifaceted approach equips students with analytical skills essential for identifying and challenging underlying ideologies and power structures in media discourse. In this way, they are prepared to become informed consumers and active participants in the global media landscape.

Challenges include limited accessibility to CDA proficiency and varying difficulty levels. Proficiency in CDA is typically associated with advanced linguistic training, limiting its accessibility for language teachers. Additionally, the difficulty of analysis varies depending on students' levels. However, despite these challenges, further research and application of CDA, combined with other analytical tools, can enhance its effectiveness, empowering students to thrive in an interconnected society.

Conclusions

The focus of this paper has been to address the educational challenges presented by the post-pandemic landscape by promoting media critical literacy through the enhancement of CLA alongside effective technology use. To this end, a synergetic framework is proposed to practically foster the development of media critical literacy skills among higher education undergraduate students by exposing them to diverse media texts and guiding them through analysis activities.

This framework offers a concrete pathway for instructors and curriculum specialists to incorporate CDA into language teaching, including an indicative course plan for implementation and examples of analysis. By applying process transitivity and appraisal analysis, students can critically assess how language is used to assign blame and responsibility, as well as to express evaluative stances in media texts, thereby gaining a nuanced understanding of the socio-political implications of language use in discourse. Through this process, students learn to deconstruct texts and interrogate the discursive strategies used by media producers to construct meaning and shape public discourse. They hence employ interpretation strategies, question dominant narratives, discern hegemonic or marginalized discourses, and uncover concealed ideologies present in various media forms. Furthermore, case studies for the analysis of crises phenomena in media have been presented, offering a critical approach for crisis communication analysis in the future.

The target demographic is primarily fourth-year English Language Teaching (ELT) university students proficient in either their first or second language and enrolled in language or media and communication courses. While university cohorts constitute the primary focus, initiating media critical literacy engagement at earlier educational stages can ensure a more comprehensive development of these critical skills, thereby better equipping individuals to evaluate media content critically from a young age (Hobbs, 2010).

Language centers must include in their mission to function as hubs for fostering critical thinking skills, dissecting media texts, and navigating the intricate landscape of language and digital media. Language educators can act as facilitators in this process, fostering critical thinking skills, guiding students through the analysis of media texts. By transcending the view of language as merely a neutral tool for communication, instructors can assist students in identifying linguistic features, discourse strategies, and rhetorical devices employed in media representations. Ultimately, incorporating critical language awareness and media literacy into school curricula is essential to prepare students for informed decision-making and active participation in a media-saturated society (Livingstone & Bulger, 2013).

References

Bednarek, M. (2006). *Evaluation in media discourse: Analysis of a newspaper corpus.* London: Continuum.

Buckingham, D. (2020). Epilogue: Rethinking Digital Literacy-Media Education in the Age of Digital Capitalism. Digital Education Review, 37, 230–239. DOI: https://doi.org/10.1344/der.2020.37.230-239

Fairclough, N. (1992a). Discourse and Social Change. Cambridge: Polity Press.

Fairclough, N. (2001). *Critical Discourse Analysis: The Critical Study of Language* (2nd ed.). Longman.

Fairclough, N. (2015). *Language and Power* (3rd ed.). Routledge.

Fowler R. (1991). Language in the news: discourse and ideology in the press. Routledge. DOI: https://doi.org/10.4324/9781315002057

Gillen, J., & Barton, D. (2010). Digital literacies: A research briefing by the Technology Enhanced Learning phase of the Teaching and Learning Research Programme. Routledge.

Godwin-Jones, R. (2020). *Emerging Technologies: Language Learning & Technology.* Language Learning & Technology, 24(3), 4–8.

Halliday M. A. K. (1994). *An Introduction to Functional Grammar.* London: Arnold.

Halliday, M. A. K., & Matthiessen, C. M. I. M. (2004). *An Introduction to Functional Grammar* (3rd Edition). London: Arnold.

Hardt-Mautner, G. (1995). *Only Connect: Critical Discourse Analysis and Corpus Linguistics.* UCREL Technical Paper 6.

Hobbs, R. (2010). *Digital and media literacy: Connecting culture and classroom.* Corwin Press.

Lave J. & Wenger-Trayner É. (2020). *Situated learning: legitimate peripheral participation.* Cambridge University Press. DOI: https://doi.org/10.1017/9781316221822

Livingstone, S., & Bulger, M. (2013). *A Global Agenda for Children's Rights in the Digital Age: Recommendations for Developing UNICEF's Research Strategy.* UNICEF Office of Research.

Martin, J. R., & White, P. R. (2005). *The language of evaluation: Appraisal in English*. Palgrave Macmillan. DOI: https://doi.org/10.1057/9780230511910

Savignon, S. J. (1987). Communicative language teaching. Theory Into Practice, *26*(4), 235–242. DOI: https://doi.org/10.1080/00405848709543281

Stockwell, P. (2021). *Language and Literature: An Introduction to Stylistics*. Routledge.

Svalberg, A. M. L. (2021). Engagement with language in relation to form-focused versus meaning-focused teaching and learning. In P. Hiver, A. H. Al-Hoorie, & S. Mercer (Eds.), *Student engagement in the language classroom* (pp. 38–55). Multilingual Matters.

Thompson, G., & Hunston, S. (2000). Evaluation: An introduction. In S. Hunston & G. Thompson (Eds.), *Evaluation in text: Authorial stance and the construction of discourse* (pp. 1–27). Oxford: Oxford University Press.

Van Dijk, T. A. (2008). *Discourse and Context: A Sociocognitive Approach*. Cambridge University Press.

Van Leeuwen, T. (2008). *Discourse and practice: New tools for critical discourse analysis*. New York: Oxford University Press. DOI: https://doi.org/10.1093/acprof:oso/9780195323306.001.0001

Wallace, C. (1992). Critical Literacy Awareness in the EFL Classroom. In N. Fairclough (Ed.), *Critical Language Awareness* (pp. 59–92). London: Longman.

Wodak, R. (2015). *The politics of fear: What right-wing populist discourses mean*. SAGE Publications. DOI: https://doi.org/10.4135/9781446270073

Databases

EBSCO Publishing (Firm). (n.d.). *Newspaper source*. Available at: http://search.ebscohost.com/login.asp?profile=web&defaultdb=nfh

Moodle. (2022). Learning Management System for Education. Retrieved from https://www.examplemoodlesite.com

Newspaper Articles (Online)

El-Erian, M. (2012, May 18). Who is to blame for Greece's crisis? *The Guardian*. Available at: https://www.theguardian.com/business/economics-blog/2012/may/18/who-blame-greece-crisis

Leader article. (2012, June 14). Armageddon ready. *The Times*. Available at: https://www.thetimes.co.uk/article/armageddon-ready-l6khb2kb38x

Ricard, P. (2013, March 6). Pas de panique, l'Europe n'est pas à l'agonie! *Le Monde*. Available at: https://www.lemonde.fr/idees/article/2013/03/06/pas-de-panique-l-europe-n-est-pas-a-l-agonie_1843752_3232.html

Websites

World Health Organization. (2020, September 23). *Managing the COVID-19 infodemic: Promoting healthy behaviours and mitigating the harm from misinformation and disinformation*. World Health Organization. https://www.who.int/news/item/23-09-2020-managing-the-covid-19-infodemic-promoting-healthy-behaviours-and-mitigating-the-harm-from-misinformation-and-disinformation

Turning Tables: Redesigning Virtual Exchange through the Learners' Experience

Laura Rampazzo, and Viviane Klen-Alves Moore

São Paulo State University (Unesp), Brazil,
and Gwinnett County Public Schools, USA
laura.rampazzo@unesp.br

Abstract

In our increasingly interconnected world, we need to effectively build relationships and communicate with people from diverse cultures and linguistic backgrounds. The Covid-19 pandemic emphasized the use of digital tools and worldwide collaboration. Tandem Learning (Brammerts, 1996) connects learners from different backgrounds to assist each other in

---

How to cite this book chapter:
Rampazzo, L. and Klen-Alves Moore, V. 2024. Turning Tables: Redesigning Virtual Exchange through the Learners' Experience. In: Athanasiou, A., Hadjiconstantinou, S. and Christoforou, M. (Eds.) *Innovative Language Teaching Practices in Higher Education in a Post-COVID Era*. Pp. 123–150. London: Ubiquity Press. DOI: https://doi.org/10.5334/bdd.g. License: CC BY 4.0

learning their languages and cultures (Telles & Vassallo, 2006). These practices have branched out from face-to-face environments to virtual exchange (VE) projects (O'Dowd, 2018). In this context, this chapter explores language learners' experiences with VE to advance programs' design and continuous development. In 2022, students from a South American institution participated in a tandem-based VE with students from North American universities. Students communicated synchronously in English and Portuguese for an extended period of time and worked in dyads to achieve the language goals they had set for themselves and complete the VE program. Following a mixed-methods approach, this study analyzes 26 learners' perspectives in a post-participation questionnaire and how these may help redesign the practice. The participants' evaluations provide valuable insights for redesigning VE projects, helping practitioners identify successful aspects to be replicated and areas needing improvement. These findings can assist other educators in promoting VEs to enhance language learning and cultural understanding.

Introduction

We live in an increasingly interconnected world in which technology plays a significant role as part of our daily lives (Cruz & Orange, 2016; Lomicka & Lorde, 2019; Moorhouse et al., 2023). To strive in this scenario, learners should be prepared to successfully establish relationships and communicate with people from diverse cultures and linguistic backgrounds (ACTFL, 2011, 2024; Brasil, 2018; Cox & Montgomery, 2019). The ramifications of such a scenario have been exacerbated during and after the global Covid-19 pandemic. People have not only become more in tune with the use of digital tools but have also been faced with the need to learn how to use them (Barbosa & Ferreira-Lopes, 2023; Lee et al., 2022; Moorhouse et al., 2023), regularly having to resort to technology for personal, business and academic purposes (Obioha et al., 2021). The pandemic heightened the critical need for worldwide collaboration, information sharing, and distribution of resources toward common goals.

One powerful tool that promotes collaboration among people from diverse backgrounds is Virtual Exchange (VE) (Dooly & Vinagre, 2020; O'Dowd, 2018, 2021). VEs have now been defined by several scholars as a result of the growing interest in their implementation (Aranha & Leone, 2017; Dooly & Vinagre, 2021; Gutierrez & O'Dowd, 2021; Leone, 2019; Oskoz & Vinagre, 2020; Vinagre & González-Lloret, 2018). The varied definitions converge into an understanding that VEs are pedagogical initiatives, commonly promoted within educational institutions and with the support of educators to connect geographically distanced learners from differing cultural backgrounds; participants work towards a common goal using a combination of synchronous and asynchronous tasks (Dooly & Vinagre, 2020; Helm 2018; Lewis & O'Dowd, 2016; O'Dowd, 2018, 2021; Sadler & Dooly, 2016). Additionally, VEs have been referred to as learner-centered practices (Dooly, 2022; Dooly & Vinagre, 2021), as they require "active participation, negotiation, problem resolution, and search for agreement" (Vinagre & González-Lloret, 2018: 4, our translation). Teachers, then, work as facilitators, guiding and supporting learners as they take charge of their learning processes in negotiation and collaboration with their peers (Cavalari & Aranha, 2019; Telles & Vassallo, 2006).

Given the increasing significance of VEs, especially in the post-Covid global landscape, and the pivotal role of learners in such practices, it is crucial to explore how participants' experiences can contribute to the advancement of these projects' design and continuous implementation. By actively seeking feedback from learners and encouraging them to reflect on their engagement, participation, and outcomes, practitioners can provide an invaluable opportunity for self-assessment and improvement. Additionally, learners' evaluations and feedback play a vital role in aligning expectations and enhancing future VEs implementations (Klen-Alves Moore, 2022).

In line with this objective, this chapter presents a mixed-methods analysis of learners' responses to a post-participation questionnaire in a VE context. The analysis focuses on data collected at the conclusion of two terms in 2022. Following this introduction, we contextualize the field of VE and explore the design principles of teletandem (Telles & Vassallo, 2006), along with its epistemological foundations and its evolution to foster language, cultural, and autonomous learning. We then delve into the pedagogical framework of teletandem, providing insights into potential redesigns based on feedback from the research participants.

Theoretical Framework

Despite the growing interest in VE, especially after the pandemic, VE had been a reality since long before Covid-19 (Stevens Initiative, 2022). The first accounts of projects that promoted online collaboration among distanced peers date to the early 1990s with the name telecollaboration (Warschauer, 1996). While such enterprises have been addressed differently, there is consensus that VE is now the preferred nomenclature (Dooly & Vinagre, 2021; O'Dowd, 2018, 2021).

The interest in VE has led to a coalition of organizations that aim to promote not only these projects but also knowledge in the field. The Stevens Initiative 2022 Report mentions several organizations, such as SUNY COIL[5] Global Network, UNICollabroation, and Red Latinoamericana COIL, among others. The teletandem network in Brazil (see teletandembrasil.org) has also significantly contributed to research on VE practices targeted at language and cultural learning (Rampazzo & Cunha, 2021).

Teletandem (Telles & Vassallo 2006) is one of the many designs VEs may undertake. It has been addressed as a VE approach to language learning (Aranha & Wigham, 2020; Barbosa & Ferreira-Lopes, 2023; Cavalari, 2018; O'Dowd, 2018) that fosters intercultural contact and autonomous learning. Inspired by tandem learning (see Tardieu & Horgues, 2019), the approach adheres to the core principles of language separation, autonomy, and reciprocity (Brammerts, 1996; Klen-Alves Moore & Rampazzo, 2023; Leone et al., 2023; Salomão et al., 2009; Vassallo & Telles, 2006). This practice operates within the framework of sociocultural theory (Telles & Vassallo, 2006), which perceives learning as a social and collaborative process unfolding through interaction within cultural contexts. It fosters language acquisition through extended VE among learners from diverse linguistic and cultural backgrounds, aligning with sociocultural theory by providing a platform for learners to engage in meaningful interactions and co-construct knowledge with their tandem partners. Through these ongoing virtual interactions, more than 8,000 learners (Brasil, 2021) have negotiated meaning as they worked together to complete tasks and develop their language skills in authentic and rich cultural contexts (Aranha & Rampazzo, 2022). In addition to prioritizing social interaction and collaboration, teletandem actively facilitates intercultural contact. Through the program,

---

[5] COIL stands for Collaborative Online International Learning. It has originated in the SUNY system and refers to a VE initiative.

learners engage with partners from diverse cultural backgrounds, gaining insights into other cultures, and the chance to navigate cultural differences (Telles et al., 2015). This VE approach can be manifested in various organizational forms, such as integration into language classes or institutional affiliations. The integrated practice (Cavalari & Aranha, 2016) promotes supported autonomous learning, which resonates with sociocultural theory and the zone of proximal development concept (Vygotsky, 1978). Within this framework, teletandem educators adopt a mediator role, gradually transferring responsibility to learners. Initially, educators provide substantial guidance and support, assisting students in setting language learning goals. Over time, learners gain confidence and independence in various tasks, empowered by the gradual transition towards greater autonomy. Throughout this process, learners continue to support each other, ensuring their mutual success (Klen-Alves Moore, 2022).

When analyzing the structure of the teletandem practice, scholars have characterized its design in terms of pedagogical and learning scenarios (Aranha & Leone, 2017). In the context of telecollaboration, the concept of a pedagogical scenario elucidates how the teletandem practice is crafted by different educators, while the learning scenario delineates how each design is implemented during the actual teletandem practice. Drawing from Aranha and Leone (2017), we argue that the design of the teletandem practice encompasses several key considerations:

- The overarching learning objectives of teletandem and the specific goals of each partnership;
- The modality of the practice, whether it is integrated into the language classroom or conducted independently;

- The interaction environment, including the tools and resources utilized to facilitate language and cultural learning, as well as to foster reflection and autonomy;
- The institutions and individuals involved in the practice, along with their respective roles and responsibilities;
- The tasks assigned to or suggested for learners to undertake during their interactions;
- The duration of each partnership and the frequency of interactions between participants.

An effective teletandem practice requires careful consideration of these factors to optimize language learning outcomes and promote meaningful intercultural exchange. To achieve this goal, the scenarios typically encompass a range of macro and micro tasks (Aranha & Leone, 2017) and a combination of synchronous and asynchronous activities for a sustained period of time. These tasks are strategically devised to support learners in achieving the project's language acquisition objectives, as well as the promotion of autonomy, reciprocity, intercultural understanding, and reflection. For example, to improve their language learning, participants engage in synchronous weekly oral sessions (Aranha & Leone, 2017) and are expected to divide the time of the interactions equally to sustain a balanced use of the languages in a partnership. Another task commonly used is the exchange of texts written in the target language. Throughout these exchanges, learners both give and receive feedback from their proficient partners, allowing them to refine their writing skills (Aranha & Cavalari, 2014).

In line with the theoretical framework of sociocultural theory, teletandem activities also include attending orientation/tutoring sessions, which prepare participants for language learning and intercultural communication while stimulating reflective abilities by prompting them to create and monitor their own language learning goals (Aranha & Cavalari, 2014). Other tasks, including learning diaries, questionnaires, and ongoing feedback (Aranha & Leone, 2017), contribute to the maintenance of autonomy and reflective practices. Moreover, mediation sessions serve as group reflection moments, guided by a mediator, where participants contemplate various aspects of language and intercultural learning (Telles, 2015). Additionally, participants often maintain learning diaries after each teletandem oral session, reflecting on their experiences and receiving feedback from educators to refine their thinking (Cavalari & Aranha, 2019, Klen-Alves Moore, 2022). Furthermore, questionnaires completed at the beginning and end of each term enable participants to express their expectations and evaluate their experiences, contributing to ongoing reflection and improvement (Aranha & Cavalari, 2014).

Overall, these tasks, as they integrate the teletandem design into pedagogical scenarios, are in line with sociocultural theory and fundamental concepts of VE, telecollaboration, and tandem learning, as they are designed to promote learners' social interaction, collaboration, autonomy, and reflection. The integration of language and intercultural learning within the teletandem practice promotes pedagogically-sound tasks that privilege active participation from learners all throughout their involvement with the project.

Methods

This study turns tables by centering students' feedback and its analysis to propose changes to the VE design. We employed a mixed-method approach to explore learners' accounts of their experiences. Through a combination of qualitative and quantitative data, we sought to provide a comprehensive assessment of participants' perspectives and evaluate the alignment between their expectations and the program's outcomes.

Research Context

Teletandem has been promoted at the campus where data has been collected since 2021. The institution is located in an inland city in the state of São Paulo, Brazil, and offers courses in secondary, technician, and higher education levels. Being a public institution, learners do not pay any tuition fee and, generally, have limited opportunities for intercultural contact or even to practice a foreign language. VE has been promoted as an extracurricular activity aimed at undergraduate and graduate students from within and outside the university. The project has followed the design described in the teletandem literature. Partnerships have been established between one language professor at the Brazilian institution and three Portuguese instructors from three universities in the United States. During their participation in 2022, learners formed pairs and exchanged their languages (Portuguese and English) and cultures over an average period of eight weeks. Before each oral session, participants were strongly encouraged to review suggestions and recommendations from previous encounters and prepare for the upcoming session.

Data Collection Procedures

Data for this study was collected through participants' responses to a structured questionnaire administered towards the end of their participation in the program. The questionnaire was sent to all participants in the program in 2022. Twenty-six voluntary undergraduate students who had fully completed the program agreed to participate in this study, providing consent to use their data for research purposes. The survey included 13 closed-ended questions and one open-ended question. It was created using a web-based survey application, and the link to it was distributed to participants via email and the learning management system platform. Additionally, participants were requested to complete the questionnaire during a final video conferencing meeting held to assess their overall experience. As participants completed the questionnaire, their responses were automatically recorded in a spreadsheet, which was subsequently anonymized to protect their identities. This instrument was used twice: first between May and June 2022 and then again in November 2022, but no participant responded to the questionnaire twice.

Instrument Development and Description

The questionnaire was carefully designed to elicit quantitative ratings and qualitative insights into participants' engagement, participation, and outcomes (refer to Appendix). Aligned with the objectives of promoting language, culture, and autonomous learning, and the study's goal of incorporating participants' perspectives into the program redesign, the questions explored learners' perceptions of intercultural contact, tasks, guidance received, and supportive learning tools. Essentially, the questionnaire was designed based on teletandem framework, as outlined earlier in our argument. The Likert scale was employed for the 13 closed-ended questions, allowing participants to indicate their level of agreement or disagreement with statements on a scale from 1 (completely disagree) to 5 (completely agree). The optional open-ended question did not impose a word limit, enabling participants to provide detailed explanations and examples based on their experiences.

Participants

The sampling procedures aimed to include a diverse group of volunteering participants from the program, considering factors such as age, reported language proficiency, and prior experience with VEs. Participants ranged in age from 17 to 40, with 11 students in their 20s, 10 in their 30s, and four in their 40s, representing diverse educational and professional backgrounds. Of the 26 undergraduate students from Brazil, 22 engaged in VE for the first time, while four had previous experience with the program. Assessing their English proficiency based on the Common European Framework of Reference for Languages (CEFR), five students self-identified as basic users, with two at level A1 and three at level A2. The majority assessed themselves at the intermediate level, with eight at B1 and nine at B2. Only three students rated themselves as proficient users at level C1, with none assessing themselves at the highest proficiency level, C2.

Data Analysis

The data analysis process involved a collaborative effort between the two authors, who manually analyzed the quantitative and qualitative data collected through a structured questionnaire. The quantitative data, gathered from the structured questionnaire, was examined using frequencies and percentages. This method provided a quantitative overview of how participants rated various aspects of the program. Simultaneously, we delved into the qualitative observation of the optional open-ended question to capture the nuanced perspectives in the post-participation questionnaire, offering deeper insights into their experiences and perceptions. Throughout the analysis, we adhered closely to the Teletandem design framework (Aranha & Leone, 2017). This framework served as a guiding structure, aligning our observations with the study's pedagogical goals and learning scenarios. By applying this theoretical framework, we ensured consistency and coherence in the analysis, enabling a comprehensive understanding of how well the program's objectives were met and the effectiveness of the tasks and resources employed.

Ethical Considerations

The study adhered to the ethical guidelines outlined by the Health Ministry (Brasil 2012)[6], ensuring that informed consent was obtained from all participants prior to data collection. Confidentiality and anonymity of participants' data were rigorously upheld throughout the research process. All gathered data were securely stored and accessible solely to the authors, safeguarding the privacy and integrity of participants.

Results

In this section, we discuss how participants' recommendations can guide future implementations of this VE, enhancing the program's alignment with learners' expectations and experiences.

---

[6] The Federal Institute of São Paulo Ethics Committee has approved the collection of data in statement number 5.393.661. (https://plata formabrasil.saude.gov.br/).

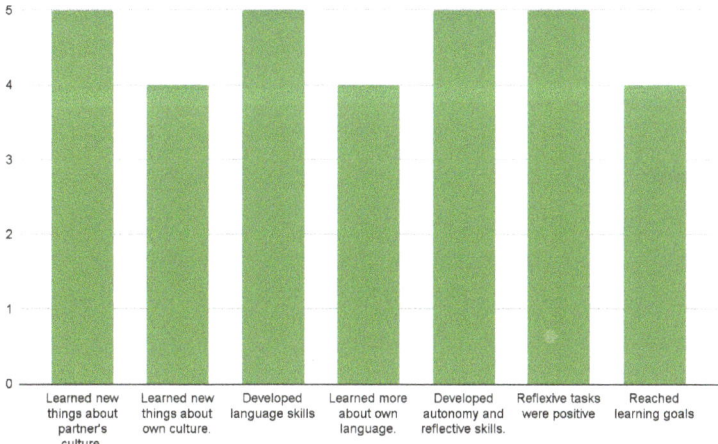

Figure 1: Participants' Perception of Their Experience.

Note: Figure 1 was created by the authors to illustrate students' perceptions regarding cultural, language, and autonomous learning.

Intercultural Knowledge and Cultural Awareness

As shown in Figure 1, when asked to reflect on intercultural knowledge (question 1) and understanding gained through the project (question 2), most participants strongly agreed (avg=4.7) that they learned new things about their partners' cultures and agreed (avg=4.0) that they gained new insights into their own culture. By assessing their cultural learning, students could evaluate how effectively teletandem facilitated intercultural understanding. They could also reflect on their own participation to confirm if they gained a deeper understanding of the other culture and if they became more self-aware of their own.

Foreign and own Language Development

Most participants strongly agreed (avg=4.6) that the VE project helped them develop their English language skills (question 3).

They also agreed (avg=3.5) that it helped them learn more about their own language (Portuguese) (question 4). By assessing the impact of the project on their foreign language proficiency, learners increased their linguistic awareness and assessed their language skills. On the same token, students evaluated the learning of their own language as they supported their international peers. Their responses indicate that the experience provided students with a deeper understanding of their native languages and increased metalinguistic knowledge.

Participants also used the open-ended question (question 14) to share that they felt their foreign language skills improved during the program and felt more confident because of teletandem. For instance, one participant noted that "it felt like the experience really helped me by developing and improving my English skills" (Male, in his twenties, response to question 14, May 11, 2022). Another participant said "it was a unique oportunite [sic] to express my english skills and pratice [sic]" (Female, in her twenties, response to question 14, December 13, 2022). A third participant shared that "this opportunity was really helpful to make myself able to achieve my personal goals regarding the English language" (Female, in her twenties, response to question 14, December 11, 2022).

Another participant mentioned, "certamente participar deste projeto foi uma excelente oportunidade para adquir [sic] mais confiança para seguir em frente na trabalhosa tarefa de aprender outro idioma" [participating in this project was definitely an excellent opportunity to gain more confidence in this hardworking task of learning another language]" (Male, in his forties, response to question 14, December 13, 2022). Participants' evaluation of the experience regarding language learning indicates that the project design is consistent with the goals of fostering language and culture learning.

Autonomy and Reflection Skills

Participants strongly agreed (avg=4.6) that they developed autonomy and reflection skills by participating in the project (question 5) and that the reflective tasks helped increase their skills and autonomy (avg= 4.5) (question 6). By evaluating the role of the tasks and their own roles as learners, students were able to recognize their growth in self-directed learning and critical thinking, contributing to their overall personal and academic development. This result highlights the program's effectiveness in fostering learner autonomy. Moreover, because learners recognize the role of the reflective tasks on their reflection skills, they acknowledge the relevance of reflecting about their tasks.

Reflecting on the mediation sessions, for instance, one participant pointed out that it would be advisable to have such sessions happening immediately after the meeting with their partners ("The only suggestion I have is, if possible, to try to do the mediation sessions after the meetings, maybe that will animate the participants to share their experiences and think about it, since they just left their meetings," female, in her twenties, response to question 14, May 11, 2022). This participant's comment indicates that she felt mediations had not been as productive/effective as they could have been if the timing had been more appropriate. On the other hand, another participant perceived the mediation sessions as essential moments for group collaboration and felt respected by his peers. In his own words,

[...] Recebi bastante apoio da mediadora do grupo de Whatsapp, [name], que sempre se mostrou muito prestativa e eficiente nas orientações. As reuniões [de mediação] com [name] foram incríveis, aprendi bastante e também usei os materiais nas atividades que desenvolvo em meu trabalho [I received a lot of support from the Whatsapp group mediator, [name], who has always been very helpful and efficient in providing guidance. The [mediation] meetings with [name] were remarkable, I learned a lot and also used the materials in my work activities]" (Male, in his forties, response to question 14, December 13, 2022)

By this apparently conflicting feedback from both learners, we conclude that participants appreciate group reflection and take upon the suggestion to have it soon after the partners' meeting, which may prove helpful in encouraging further participants' engagement.

Goal Achievement

When reflecting on the goals set at the beginning of the project, participants (avg=4.4) agreed that they had reached their learning goals (question 7). This question enables learners to assess the alignment between their expectations and the actual outcomes, providing insights into the project's success through the individuals meeting their learning objectives.

Figure 2 illustrates participants' insights on the VE design when answering if the topics or tasks proposed for the oral sessions were useful and appropriate (question 9), if the synchronous and asynchronous tasks took too much time to be completed (question 10), and if Canvas, the platform selected to mediate their learning, was easy to use (question 11).

The Usefulness of Suggested Topics/Tasks

Participants strongly agreed that the topics and tasks suggested for the oral session were valuable and appropriate (avg=4.6). No participant included additional comments on the tasks, suggesting they were appropriate. This positive result indicates that the

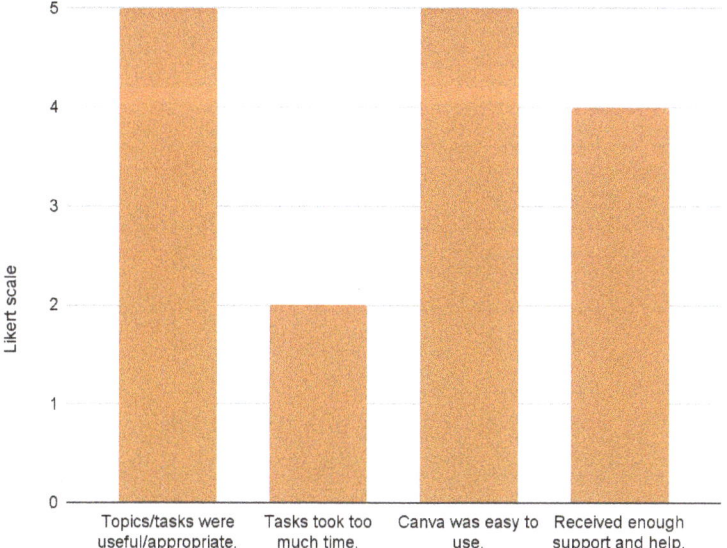

Figure 2: Participants' Evaluation of Project Components.

Note: Figure 2 was created by the authors to illustrate participants' evaluation of the tasks, platforms, and support they received.

instructional materials are aligned with the learners' needs and that there is no need for changes in topics and tasks. Nevertheless, future applications of the questionnaire could include a mandatory open-ended question in which participants could elaborate more on the usefulness of suggested topics and tasks.

Time Commitment for Project Tasks

Participants disagree (avg=2.4) that tasks take too much time. Thus, both synchronous and asynchronous tasks require an appropriate amount of time. This result helps us confirm that the workload of 15–18 hours was reasonable and manageable throughout the 7–9 weeks they were expected to commit to the project.

Had the results been different, adjusting tasks and teaching time management strategies to the students would be necessary.

Usability of the Canvas Platform

Students strongly agree that Canvas was easy to use (avg=4.6). When choosing an online learning environment to host VE, it is essential to evaluate it to confirm its user-friendliness and accessibility. By evaluating the ease of use of the Canvas platform in the closed-ended question, participants gave us insight into the accessibility of the platform used. Since no participant suggested using a different platform nor commented on having difficulties using it, there is no need for additional technical support. Similar to the comment above on their evaluation of the tasks, a mandatory open-ended question for participants to describe their experience with the platform might be useful.

Assessing Support and Assistance

When assessing the level of support and assistance provided, participants generally agreed (average rating of 4.4) that they received sufficient help from the project coordinator and assistants. However, some participants did not strongly agree, citing instances where their individual needs were not addressed promptly, such as when a partner abruptly withdrew from the program. While most participants expressed gratitude for the team's support, one student highlighted the lack of feedback regarding the partner's absence, which indicates the importance of maintaining consistent communication with students and their counterparts abroad to ensure retention and promptly address dropouts. Taking the participants' feedback into account allows for improvements in future projects by enhancing the provision of guidance and assistance. To address unexpected situations and enhance participants' understanding of the nature of virtual partnerships, we could create a manual with a thorough explanation of recurrent problems, improving the overall learning experience in VE programs.

Evaluating the Duration of the Project

Despite not being explicitly addressed in the closed-ended questions, participants' comments about the project length were observed in their responses to the open-ended question. Several learners expressed a desire for more meetings with their partners, implying that they would have valued an extended project duration. It is important to acknowledge this feedback as a valid input. However, it should be noted that not all participants' suggestions can directly inform project redesign due to practical and institutional constraints. Challenges such as the variations in academic calendars, which limit the project's length, may pose functional obstacles and restrictions that are difficult to overcome. Therefore, while acknowledging the desire for a longer project duration, it is crucial to weigh practical considerations when determining the optimal length of a VE project. These considerations may include logistical feasibility[7] and the project's specific learning objectives. Balancing these factors ensures that the VE project remains sustainable and effective in achieving its educational goals.

---

[7] In this context, logistical feasibility refers to taking into account institutional calendars, number of participants, the necessary resources, and infrastructure available.

Discussion

The findings underscore the importance of participants' evaluations of VE in informing project redesign efforts and enabling practitioners to identify successful elements for replication and areas necessitating reconsideration. Participants' responses acknowledge the program's efficacy in fostering language, intercultural, and reflective autonomous learning (Klen-Alves Moore & Rampazzo, 2023; Leone et al., 2023; Salomão et al. 2009; Vassallo & Telles, 2006), that is, the framework of tasks used (Aranha & Leone, 2017) seems to have contributed to gains in language, intercultural and reflective learning.

Corroborating Klen-Alves Moore's (2022) arguments, learners' answers also pinpoint areas for improvement. Participants' suggestions for scheduling mediation sessions promptly after partner interactions and optimizing session calendars for increased semester engagement may be taken into consideration by educators in promoting future exchanges. Given the significance of VE in our increasingly digital, post-pandemic globalized world, promoting VEs is an essential step to fostering intercultural education and facilitating participants' learning. By incorporating learners' evaluation and perspectives, we can cater to their needs and enhance the experience.

Conclusion

This chapter discussed the pivotal role of investigating learners' responses in shaping the redesign of VE projects. While our analysis stems from a specific project design, we contend that the insights gleaned offer a roadmap for integrating a learner-centered approach across diverse VE initiatives, thus presenting invaluable prospects for improving and enhancing VE implementation.

There are potential limitations of this work, the first is regarding generalizability. The investigation relied on questionnaires as the data collection instrument, which limited students' responses and evaluations. Second, the study considered limited space and data. In the cut made, we may have explored only some potential factors influencing learners' responses extensively. Integrating observational data could have offered further insights from the instructors' standpoint, enriching our discussion of the VE dynamics.

Future research could employ diverse data collection methods, such as gathering data from participants on both sides of the exchange, conducting semi-structured interviews, and analyzing learners' weekly responses to reflective diary prompts. Additionally, incorporating instructor perspectives through the analysis of classroom observations, email exchanges, project design documents, and interviews could offer a more nuanced understanding of VE dynamics and different implementation strategies.

References

ACTFL. (2011). 21st century skills map. Retrieved from https://www.actfl.org/uploads/files/general/Documents/21st _Century_Skills_Map.pdf. Access on June 06th, 2023.

ACTFL. (2024). Proficiency Guidelines. Retrieved from https://www.actfl.org/uploads/files/general/Resources-Publications /ACTFL_Proficiency_Guidelines_2024.pdf. Access on June 22nd, 2024.

Aranha, S., & Cavalari, S. M. S. (2014). A trajetória do projeto Teletandem Brasil: da modalidade Institucional Não-Integrada à Institucional Integrada. *The ESPecialist, 35*(2), 183–201.

Aranha, S., & Leone, P. (2017). The development of DOTI (Databank of oral teletandem oral interaction). In D, Fisher, & M. Beibwenger (Eds.), *Investigating computer-mediated communication corpus-based approaches to language in the digital world* (pp. 172–190). 1st ed. Ljubljana University Press, Faculty of Arts.

Aranha, S., & Rampazzo, L. (2022). Towards a Working Definition of Negotiation in Telecollaboration: Analysis of Teletandem oral sessions. *Colombian Applied Linguistics Journal, 24*(2), 234–245.

Aranha, S., & Wigham, C. R. (2020). Virtual exchanges as complex research environments: facing the data management challenge. A case study of Teletandem Brasil. *Journal of Virtual Exchange, 3*, 13–38. DOI: https://doi.org/10.21827/jve.3.35748

Barbosa, M. W., & Ferreira-Lopes, L. (2023). Emerging trends in telecollaboration and virtual exchange: a bibliometric study. *Educational Review, 75*(3), 558–586. DOI: https://doi.org/10.1080/00131911.2021.1907314

Benedetti, A. M. (2010). Dos princípios de tandem ao Teletandem. In A. M. Benedetti, D. A. Consolo, & M. H. Vieira-Abrahão (Ed.). *Pesquisas em ensino e aprendizagem no Teletandem Brasil*: Línguas estrangeiras para todos (pp. 21–45). Campinas: Pontes Editores.

Brasil. Ministério da Educação. (2018). Base Curricular Nacional Comum. MEC.

Brasil. Ministério da Saúde. (2012). Resolução nº 466, de 12 de dezembro de 2012.

Brasil. Ministério das Relações Exteriores. (2021). *Panorama da contribuição do Brasil para a difusão do português*. Brasília: FUNAG.

Cappellini, M., Elstermann, A. K., & Rivens Mompean, A. (2020). Reciprocity 2.0: How reciprocity is mediated through different formats of learners' logs. In C. Horgues, & C. Tardieu A (Ed.). *Redefining Tandem Language and Culture Learning in Higher Education*, Paris: Routledge.

Cavalari, S. M. S. (2018). Integrating telecollaborative language learning into Higher Education: a study on teletandem practice. *BELT. Brazilian English Language Teaching Journal, 9*(2), 417–432. DOI: https://doi.org/10.15448/2178-3640.2018.2.31927

Cavalari, S. M. S., & Aranha, S. (2016). Teletandem: Integrating e-learning into the foreign language classroom. *Acta Scientiarum: Language and Culture, 38*(4), 327–336.

Cavalari, S. M. S., & Aranha, S. (2019). The Teacher's Role in Telecollaborative Language Learning: The Case of Institutional Integrated Teletandem. *Revista Brasileira de Linguística Aplicada, 19*(3), 555–578. DOI: https://doi.org/10.1590/1984-6398201913576

Cox, C. B., & Montgomery, C. (2019). A study of 21st century skills and engagement in a university Spanish foreign language classroom. *Foreign Language Annals, 2*, 822–849. DOI: https://doi.org/10.1111/flan.12426

Cruz, M., & Orange, E. (2016). 21st Century Skills In The Teaching Of Foreign Languages At Primary And Secondary Schools. *TOJET: The Turkish Online Journal of Educational Technology, Special Issue*, 1–12.

Cavalari, S. M. S., & Aranha, S. (2016). Teletandem: Integrating e-learning into the foreign language classroom. *Acta Scientiarum: Language and Culture, 38*(4), 327–336.

Dooly, M. (2022). The evolution of virtual exchange and assessment practices. In A. Czura & M. Dooly (Eds), *Assessing virtual exchange in foreign language courses at tertiary level* (pp. 13–27). Research-publishing.net. DOI: https://doi.org/10.14705/rpnet.2022.59.1407

Dooly, M., & Vinagre, M. (2021). Research into practice: Virtual exchange in language teaching and learning. *Language Teaching*, 1–15. DOI: https://doi.org/10.1017/S0261444821000069

Gutiérrez, B. F., & O'Dowd, R. (2021). Virtual exchange: connecting language learners in online intercultural collaborative learning. In T. Beaven & F. Rosell-Aguilar (Eds), *Innovative language pedagogy report* (pp. 17–22). Researchpublishing.net. DOI: https://doi.org/10.14705/rpnet.2021.50.1230

Helm, F. (2018). *Emerging Identities in Virtual Exchange*. Voillans: Research-publishing.net. DOI: https://doi.org/10.14705/rpnet.2018.25.9782490057191

Lee, J., Leibowitz, J., & Rezek, J. (2022). The Impact of International Virtual Exchange on Participation in Education Abroad. *Journal of Studies in International Education, 26*(2), 202–221. DOI: https://doi.org/10.1177/10283153211052

Leone, P. (2017). Migrazioni virtual: teletandem per l'apprendimento di una L2. *Incontri. Revista europea di studi italiani, 31*(2), 61–78. DOI: https://doi.org/10.18352/incontri.10171

Leone, P., Aranha, S., & Cavalari, S. M. S. (2023). 'Our interaction was very productive': levels of reflection in learners' diaries in teletandem. *Alsic [En ligne], Textes à paraître dans le prochain volume*, Recherche, mis en ligne le 01 février 2023, consulté le 20 juin 2023. http://journals.openedition.org/alsic/6459

Lewis, T., & O'Dowd, R. (2016). Online Intercultural Exchange and Foreign Language Learning: A Systematic Review. In: R. O'Dowd, R.; T. Lewis. (Eds.), *Online intercultural exchange*: Policy, pedagogy, practice (pp. 29–72). Routledge.

Lomicka, L., & Lord, G. (2019). Reframing Technology's Role in Language Teaching: A Retrospective Report. *Annual Review of Applied Linguistics*, 1–16.

Lopes, Q. B. (2019). *MulTeC*: A construção de um corpus multimodal em teletandem. [Doctoral dissertation, Universidade Estadual Paulista 'Júlio de Mesquita Filho', São José do Rio Preto].

Klen-Alves Moore, V. S. (2022). *Implementing telecollaboration in the world language classroom* [Doctoral dissertation, University of Georgia]. ProQuest Dissertations and Theses Global. https://esploro.libs.uga.edu/esploro/outputs/9949450324302959

Klen-Alves Moore, V. S., & Rampazzo, L. (2023). Teletandem principles in focus: Documenting how learners act during the oral sessions. *Revista (Con)Textos Linguísticos, 17*(38), 182–202.

Moorhouse, B. L., Kohnke, L., & Wan, Y. (2023). A Systematic Review of Technology Reviews in Language Teaching and Learning Journals. *RELC Journal*, 1–19. DOI: https://doi.org/10.1177/00336882221150

Obioha, B.; Udeh, K. N. & Izunwanne, G. N. (2021). Global Communications in Covid-19 Pandemic Era: A Theoretical Review of the Anxieties and Role of ICTS/Social Media, *ANSU Journal of Arts and Social Sciences, (ANSUJASS), 8*(2), 73–96.

O'Dowd, R. (2018). From telecollaboration to virtual exchange: state-of-the-art and the role of UNICollaboration in moving forward. *Journal of Virtual Exchange, 1,* 1–23. DOI: https://doi.org/10.14705/rpnet.2018.jve.1

O'Dowd, R. (2021). Virtual Exchange: moving forward into the next decade. *Computer Assisted Language Learning,* 1–17. DOI: https://doi.org/10.1080/09588221.2021.1902201

Oskoz, A., & Vinagre, M. (Eds.). (2020). *Understanding Attitude in Intercultural Virtual Communication.* Equinox Publishing.

Picoli, F., & Salomão, A. C. B. (2020). O princípio da separação de línguas no Teletandem: o que as teorias propõem e como ele funciona na prática. *Revista Estudos Linguísticos, 49*(3), 1605–1623. DOI: https://doi.org/10.21165/el.v49i3.2458

Rampazzo, L. (2021). *Gêneros do intercâmbio virtual*: recorrência retórica e uso de polidez no primeiro encontro síncrono. [Doctoral dissertation, Universidade Estadual Paulista 'Júlio de Mesquita Filho']. http://hdl.handle.net/11449/210956

Rampazzo, L., & Cunha, J. N. C. (2021). Telecollaborative practice in Brazil: What has been published about teletandem?. *BELT – Brazilian English Language Teaching Journal,* 12(1), e40023. DOI: https://doi.org/10.15448/2178-3640.2021.1.40023

Sadler, R., & Dooly, M. (2016). Twelve years of telecollaboration: what we have learnt. *ELT Journal, 70*(4), 401–413. DOI: https://doi.org/10.1093/elt/ccw041

Stevens Initiative. (2022). *2022 Survey of the Virtual Exchange Field Report.* Washington: The Aspen Institute. https://www.stevensinitiative.org/wp-content/uploads/2022/11/2022-Survey-of-the-Virtual-Exchange-Field-Report.pdf

Telles, J. A. (2015). Learning foreign languages in teletandem: Resources and strategies. *DELTA: Documentação de Estudos em Linguística Teórica e Aplicada, 31*(3), 603–632. DOI: https://doi.org/10.1590/0102-4450226475643730772

Telles, J. A., & Vassallo, M. L. (2006). Foreign language learning in-tandem: Teletandem as an alternative proposal in CALLT. *The ESPecialist, 27*(2), 189–212.

Telles, J. A., Zakir, M. A., & Funo, L. B. A. (2015). Teletandem e episódios relacionados a cultura. *DELTA: Documentação de Estudos em Linguística Teórica e Aplicada, 31*(2), 359–389.

Vinagre, M., & González-Lloret, M. (2018). La comunicación mediada por computador y su integración en el aprendizaje de segundas lenguas. In M. González-Lloret, & M. Vinagre, (Eds.), *Comunicación mediada por tecnologías*: Aprendizaje y Enseñanza de la Lengua Extranjera (pp. 1–19). Equinox Publishing.

Vygotsky, L. (1978). *Mind in society.* Cambridge: Harvard University Press.

Warschauer, M. (1996). *Telecollaboration in foreign language learning*: proceedings of the Hawaii Symposium. Honolulu, HI: University of Hawaii Second Language Teaching and Curriculum Center.

Appendix

Questionnaire administered to the participants towards the end of two terms in 2022

Demographics

How old are you? ( ) 17–19; ( ) 20–29; ( ) 30–39; ( ) 40–49; ( ) 50–59; ( ) 60–69

What is your gender? ( ) Female; ( ) Male; ( ) Non-binary; ( ) Other; ( ) I would rather not say

How do you assess your ability in English? (Based on https://www.britishcouncil.org.br/quadro-comum-europeu-de-referencia-para-linguas-cefr)
( ) A1; ( ) A2; ( ) B1; ( ) B2; ( ) C1; ( ) C2

You are an undergraduate student at [opens list of options]

You will get a degree on [opens list of options]
In which group did you participate? [opens list of options]
Was this your first time participating in a virtual exchange project/program? ( ) Yes ( ) No

Assessment of the experience

For the next questions, rate your level of agreement with each statement (1= completely disagree; 2= disagree; 3= neither agree nor disagree; 4= agree; 5= completely agree)

1. **I feel I learned new things about my partner's culture.**
   Completely disagree ( ) 1 ( ) 2 ( ) 3 ( ) 4 ( ) 5 Completely agree

2. **I feel I learned new things about my own culture.**
   Completely disagree ( ) 1 ( ) 2 ( ) 3 ( ) 4 ( ) 5 Completely agree

3. **I feel the project helped me develop my language skills in English.**
   Completely disagree ( ) 1 ( ) 2 ( ) 3 ( ) 4 ( ) 5 Completely agree

4. **I feel I learned new things about my own language.**
   Completely disagree ( ) 1 ( ) 2 ( ) 3 ( ) 4 ( ) 5 Completely agree

5. **I feel I developed some autonomy and reflection skills.**
   Completely disagree ( ) 1 ( ) 2 ( ) 3 ( ) 4 ( ) 5 Completely agree

6. **I feel the reflection tasks helped me develop some autonomy and reflection skills.**
   Completely disagree ( ) 1 ( ) 2 ( ) 3 ( ) 4 ( ) 5 Completely agree

7. **I feel I reached my learning goals (Check the goals you set at the beginning of the project).**
   Completely disagree ( ) 1 ( ) 2 ( ) 3 ( ) 4 ( ) 5 Completely agree

8. **I feel the suggested topics or tasks for the oral sessions with my partner(s) were useful/appropriate.**
   Completely disagree ( ) 1 ( ) 2 ( ) 3 ( ) 4 ( ) 5 Completely agree

9. **I feel the project tasks (synchronous and asynchronous ones) took too much time.**
   Completely disagree ( ) 1 ( ) 2 ( ) 3 ( ) 4 ( ) 5 Completely agree

10. **I feel the Canvas platform was easy to use.**
    Completely disagree ( ) 1 ( ) 2 ( ) 3 ( ) 4 ( ) 5 Completely agree

11. **I would like to keep in touch with my partner(s).**
    Completely disagree ( ) 1 ( ) 2 ( ) 3 ( ) 4 ( ) 5 Completely agree

12. **I feel I received enough support and help from the project coordinator and assistants.**
    Completely disagree ( ) 1 ( ) 2 ( ) 3 ( ) 4 ( ) 5 Completely agree

13. **I would like to participate in the project again in the future.**
    Completely disagree ( ) 1 ( ) 2 ( ) 3 ( ) 4 ( ) 5 Completely agree

14. **Please, use this space to add any reflections, suggestions, complaints.**

Contributors

Androulla Athanasiou is an English Language Instructor at the Language Centre of the Cyprus University of Technology (CUT). She holds an MA in English and Language Studies and Methods from Warwick University (2000), an MA in Educational Leadership from the European University Cyprus (2012) and a PhD in English Language Teaching from Warwick University (2005). Her research interests lie in material design, the use of technology in language teaching/learning (Computer Assisted Language Learning), learner autonomy, collaborative learning, the use of Common European Framework of References for Languages (CEFR). ORCID: https://orcid.org/0000-0002-0125-8033

Jack Burston holds the position of Honorary Research Fellow in the Language Centre of the Cyprus University of Technology. He is a language-teaching specialist with a formal background in theoretical and applied linguistics, second language acquisition and testing. His current research is focused on Mobile-Assisted Language Learning (MALL) and advanced-level foreign language instruction. Jack is a current member of the Editorial Board of the ReCALL Journal, Language Learning & Technology Journal and The Journal of Teaching English with Technology. He also served for many years on the Editorial Board of the CALICO Journal and was the Software Review Editor of the CALICO Journal for 13 years. ORCID: https://orcid.org/0000-0003-2905-5585

Eirini Busack is employed as a research assistant in the English Department of the Karlsruhe University of Education in Germany since April 2022. She holds a Bachelor of Arts degree in Education sciences from the Aegean University in Greece and an M.A. in Computer-Assisted Language Learning from the Cyprus University of Technology in Limassol. Additionally, she holds an M.Sc. in Immersive Technologies from the International Hellenic University and an M.A. in Specialised Translation from the University of Roehampton in the UK. Her research interests encompass: E-Learning, adaptive learning, immersive technologies, teacher training education, Computer-Assisted Language Learning, and Mobile-Assisted Language Learning. ORCID: https://orcid.org/0009-0000-7946-5334

Maria Christoforou is a PhD Candidate, focusing on the pedagogical affordances of Virtual Reality in the learning of English as a foreign language. She has a Master's degree in Applied Linguistics from the Open University, UK and a Bachelor's degree in English Language and Literature from the University of Cyprus. She is involved in curriculum development and teaching of English for Specific Purposes at the Cyprus University of Technology Language Centre and implements Virtual Reality and Mixed

Reality technologies in her courses. She has received research grants for collaboration with the Language Centre of Taipei Medical University, Taiwan, and has also organised intercultural projects via High Immersion Social Virtual Reality with Utrecht University, Netherlands. Her research interests revolve around Virtual Reality-Assisted Language Learning (VRALL), immersive technologies, and multimodality. ORCID: https://orcid.org/0000-0001-7598-6159

Dana Di Pardo Léon-Henri is a senior researching lecturer with ELLIADD (EA 4661) and a tenured Associate Professor at the University of Franche-Comté in Besançon, France, where she teaches English for Specific Purposes (ESP). She holds a PhD in Applied Linguistics from the University of La Sorbonne, Paris, and a Bachelor of Arts in French and Italian from Brock University. Her research focuses on ESP and Language for Specific Purposes (LSP) teaching, foreign language pedagogy, evaluation, and the role of artificial intelligence in education. She has published several books and articles in peer-reviewed journals and presented her research at various international conferences. Her teaching philosophy emphasizes active engagement, critical thinking, inclusivity, skill development, and holistic growth for students. ORCID: https://orcid.org/0000-0001-6196-6173

Dia Evagorou holds a PhD in Language, Discourse, and Communication from King's College London. Her doctoral research focused on combining corpus tools and discourse-analytical approaches to examine language use in media communication. The research is conducted using a mixed-method approach and involves analysing data from many languages. Her primary research interests focus on Discourse Analysis, Linguistics, and

Communication, interdisciplinary applications of Discourse Analysis (specifically examining the relationship between language and ideology in various communicational contexts), strategic and corporate communication, and critical linguistic awareness in education. She has taught Greek as a foreign language to students and adults through the Ministry of Education Programs. In addition, she has had positions as an editor in many Cypriot media outlets, focusing on language, education, and culture. ORCID: https://orcid.org/0000-0001-8031-2765

Stavroulla Hadjiconstantinou is a member of the Special Teaching Staff at the Language Centre of Cyprus University of Technology (CUT) since 2009. She holds a Bachelor's degree in Language Studies and a Master's degree in Applied linguistics both from Essex University, UK. Stavroulla also holds a PhD in Linguistics and English Language from Lancaster University UK. Her research interests include Second language acquisition, ESP curriculum and material design and development, Pedagogical applications of Critical thinking in Education, Technology Enhanced Language Learning, Multimodality and Digital media literacy. ORCID: https://orcid.org/0000-0001-6226-8000

Elis Kakoulli Constantinou is the Deputy Director of the Language Centre of the Cyprus University of Technology, where she teaches English. She is also the coordinator of the Distance Learning Group of the Cyprus University of Technology Learning Development Network and a teacher trainer at the Cyprus Pedagogical Institute of the Ministry of Education, Culture, Sports and Youth. She holds a PhD specialising in English for Specific Purposes Teacher Education (Cyprus University of Technology), an MA in Applied Linguistics (University of Essex, UK) and a BA in English Language and Literature (National and Kapodistrian University of Athens, Greece). Her research focuses on English for Specific Purposes, Teacher Education, Curriculum Development, Teaching Methodology, Technology Enhanced Language Learning and Action Research. ORCID: https://orcid.org/0000-0001-8854-3816

Viviane Klen-Alves Moore is a Parent Instructional Coordinator at Baldwin Elementary within Gwinnett County Public Schools, where she plays a pivotal role in Family Engagement, offering building capacity training to ensure parents are involved and have the tools to support their children's education. She holds a Doctorate in Language and Literacy Education and a Master's in Romance Languages from the University of Georgia (US). She specialized in TESOL and World Languages Education, concentrating in Portuguese, Spanish, and English. She has invested substantial time in teaching world languages and researching the integration of virtual exchange in the language classroom, discussing virtual exchange concepts and practices in her courses, publications, and presentations. ORCID: https://orcid.org/0000-0001-7601-9259

Cíntia Rabello holds a BA in Languages (Portuguese-English), a Master's Degree in Educational Technology and a PhD in Applied Linguistics. She is an Adjunct Professor of English Language in the Department of Modern Foreign Languages at the Institute of Letters at Universidade Federal Fluminense (UFF) in Rio de Janeiro, Brazil, and a researcher in the Graduate Program in Language Studies at the same university. She is a member of the colearning network of the Open University – UK and of the Special Interest Group on Language and Technology of the National

Association of Graduate Programs and Research on Letters and Liguistics (ANPOLL). Her research interests comprise English language teaching, CALL, language teacher education, digital technologies, digital literacies, multiliteracies, and digital education. ORCID: https://orcid.org/0000-0002-3811-4228

Laura Rampazzo is an Assistant Professor at the Department of Modern Languages at São Paulo State University (2024–Present). She holds a Masters (2017) and a Doctorate (2021) degree in Linguistics. She has a teaching degree in Languages (Portuguese and English) from São Paulo State University (2014). She worked at the Federal Institute of São Paulo (2017–2024), where she taught Portuguese and English at the Secondary, Technician, and Higher Education levels. She is committed to creating opportunities for students to engage in intercultural contact and designing and running virtual exchange projects. Her research interests include language teaching, virtual exchange/telecollaboration, genres, communities, and linguistic politeness. ORCID: https://orcid.org/0000-0002-4736-9900

Index

A

agency and its linguistic manifestations
  Critical Discourse Analysis   106, **107**–120
  ideational meaning   106
  material processes   108
    empowering participants   108–109
  mental processes   109
  organised learning   85
  relational processes   109
  verbal processes   108
    empowering participants   107–159
AI-related technologies   52, 68
asynchronous approach to instruction   5
cloud technologies   36
digital learning paths and flipped classroom combinations   74, 84, 85
flipped classroom learning   78
Google Workspace for Education   **40**–**47**
interpersonal and community learning   86–89
teletandem practice   129
Virtual Exchange   125
  time commitment   139
autonomy. *See* learner autonomy

C

CALL teacher education
practices   2, 9
  case study   14–24
  concerns   10–11
  emergency remote teaching
    and learning   15–20,
    17, 23
  language teacher education
    curricula   11–13
  relevance of elective discipline
    14, 15–17, 22
challenges faced in language
  learning and teaching
  contexts   29, 32–35, 37
  COVID-19, impact of   1–5,
    49–50, 50–51, 50–52, 52,
    97, 98, 99
  Critical Discourse Analysis
    98–100, 117–118
  Critical Language Awareness
    and use of technology
    99–100, 117–119
  digital inequalities and
    exclusion   17, 18,
    22, 25
  digital literacies   11–13
  emergency remote teaching
    and learning   10, 14,
    16–17
  technological
    advancements   49,
    50–51, 52–53, 99
cloud technologies   4–7
  English for Specific Purposes
    courses   35
  Google Workspace for
    Education   36–37
  transversal skills,
    development of
    38–58
  See also Google Workspace
    for Education   43
cognitive skills
  academic "cognitive" skills
    3, 29
  Critical Language
    Awareness   99
    Systemic Functional
      Grammar model
      of meanings   101
  development   31
  English for Specific Purposes
    courses   32
    Google Workspace for
      Education
      37, 38
  metacognitive awareness
    53, 62–63, 65
  reflective writing
    53–54, 66–68
collaborative learning   5–6,
  33–34, 79, 88, 103, 127
  Google Workspace for
    Education   **39, 40**
  communication skills   51
  Critical Discourse Analysis
    117–118
  Critical Language Awareness
    99
  digital learning paths and
    flipped classroom
    combinations   74, 78, 90

organised learning   85
English for Specific Purposes courses   32–33, 35–36
reflective writing   51, 53–54
connectivist approach to learning   31, 36
Critical Discourse Analysis (CDA)   98, 100
  challenges   98–100, 117–118
  integration into classroom environment   5, **103**, 106, 117–129
  integration into language teaching   118
  interpersonal meanings   112–120
  linguistic manifestations of agency   106–121
  Systemic Functional Grammar model of meanings   101–102
Critical Language Awareness (CLA)   6–9, 97, 99, 118
critical thinking skills   6, 34, 119
cultural awareness   50, 54, 65, 135

D

dialogic learning   86
diary share   56
digital inequalities and exclusion   3, 17, 18, 22, 25
digital learning paths and flipped classroom combinations   4–5, 73, 90–91
  asynchronous and synchronous approaches to learning   74–78
    asynchronous learning   84
    remote synchronous delivery   78
    synchronous learning   83
  case study   81–88
  communication and social needs
    dialogic learning   86–87
    interpersonal and community learning   86–89
    organised learning   85
  digital learning paths   79–80, 82
  flipped classroom   78
  grammatical knowledge   85
  online course evaluation   85–89
digital literacies   2, 10, 14
  CALL teacher education practices   10–11, 24–25
  emergency remote teaching and learning   22, 23
  language teacher education curricula   11–13
  public policy   17
  See also CALL teacher education practices   23

E

educational and personal growth 49
  reflective writing 4, 49–50, 55–57, 68
    case study 57–68
emergency remote education (ERE). *See* emergency remote teaching and learning (ERTL)
emergency remote teaching and learning (ERTL) 2, 77
  CALL teacher education 10
  challenges faced in language learning and teaching contexts 10, 14, 16–17
  digital literacies 22, 23
  English for Specific Purposes (ESP) courses 29
  Google Workspace for Education **40–47**
  transdisciplinarity and transversalilty 32–35
European Union
  importance of transversal skills 27, 30, 42

F

flipped classroom learning 4, 78
  See also digital learning paths and flipped classroom combinations 90

G

global interconnectedness 50–51, 118, 124–126
goal achievement
  agency and its linguistic manifestations 107–159
  cognitive skills development 31, 42, 80
  self-discipline 55
  transitivity patterns 111
  Virtual Exchange 128–130, 138
Google Workspace for Education 36–42, 43
  English for Specific Purposes courses **40–47**
  motivation of students 37, 38, 42
  Project-Based Language Learning **39–58**
  transversal skills, development of 38–58

I

ideational meaning 102, 117
  linguistic representations of agency 106
information and communications technologies (ICT) 117
  English for Specific Purposes courses 35, 35–37
intercultural knowledge 4, 6, 50, 54, 65, 135, 142
interpersonal and community learning 86–89

interpersonal meanings 102, 117
   appraisal categories **112–118**
      application 113–116

L

language development
   Virtual Exchange 135–136
language proficiency 28, 32, 133
language separation
   Virtual Exchange 127
learner autonomy 4, 35, 42
   English for Specific Purposes courses 33–35
      Google Workspace for Education 38–58
   Project Based Language Learning 31–32, 37, 43
   reflective writing 137
   teletandem activities 129
   Virtual Exchange 127, 137–138
life writing 56–57
   See also reflective writing 137

M

media literacy 5, 98–99
   critical language awareness, importance of 97, 100, 117–118, 119
mediation 142
   group reflection 130, 137–138
metacognitive skills 31, 49
   independence and resilience 51, 53
   reflective writing 62, 66–68
Mobile-Assisted Language Learning (MALL) practices 24
motivation of students
   Google Workspace for Education 37, 38, 42
   interactivity 79, 88
"non-academic" skills and competencies 3, 29
   See also transversal skills

O

organised learning 85

P

problem-solving 30, 31, 33, 54
Project-Based Language Learning (PBLL) 31, 34, 42
   cloud technologies 35–37
   learner autonomy 37

R

reciprocity
   Virtual Exchange 127
reflective writing 50–51
   communication skills 51, 53–54
   educational and personal growth 4, 49–50, 55–57, 68
      case study 57
   learner autonomy 137

reflective writing *(continued)*
  life writing   56–57
  metacognitive
      awareness   53, 62, 67
  post-COVID global
      transformations   52–53
  self-regulation   54, 66, 66–67
  teletandem activities   130
  transversal skills   54
  Virtual Exchange   137–138
remote synchronous delivery
    (RSD)   77–78, 78, 88–89

S

self-regulation   49, 51, 53, 54,
    61, 66
reflective writing   4, 66–67
social constructivist approach
    to learning   31, 36
sociocultural theory
  teletandem activities   127,
    129–130
soft skills. *See* transversal skills
student engagement
    34–35, 68
  collaborative learning   79
  Critical Discourse
      Analysis   100
  Critical Language
      Awareness   99
  digital learning paths and
      flipped classroom
      combinations   90
  remote synchronous
      delivery   88
  Virtual Exchange   126, 132

synchronous approach to
    instruction   5
  cloud technologies   36
  dialogic learning   86
  flipped classroom
      learning   78
  Google Workspace for
      Education   **40–47**
  interpersonal and
      community
      learning   86–89
  remote synchronous
      delivery   77
  teletandem practice   129
  Virtual Exchange   125
      time commitment   139
Systemic Functional Grammar
    (SFG)   98
  integration into classroom
      environment   117
  model of meanings   101–102

T

tandem learning   123, 130
  sociocultural theory   127–130
  See also teletandem
      activities   136
teacher-guided learning   34
teaching methods
  COVID-19, impact of   52
  teamwork   29, 33, 53, 89
  technological advancements
  COVID-19, impact of   49,
      50–51, 52–53, 99
  teletandem activities   7, 126,
      127–130, 129, 130, 131

learner autonomy 129
reflective writing 130
Virtual Exchange 134, 135, 136
textual meaning 102, 117
transdisciplinary knowledge 29, 30–32
  English for Specific Purposes courses 32–35
transitivity patterns
  agency 106
  evaluative language 102, 118
  perspective and presentation 110
  social actor representation 101
transversal skills 4, 28, 42
  categories 30
  development of 28–29, 30–32
    Google Workspace for Education 37, 38–58
  English for Specific Purposes courses 3, 27, 29, 32–35
  language learning 29–32
  reflective writing 54

U

UNESCO
  importance of transversal skills 28, 29–30, 42

V

Virtual Exchange (VE) 125, 126–128, 142
  cultural awareness 135
  intercultural knowledge 135
  language development 135–136
  language learning, approach to 6–7, 127–130
  learner autonomy 127, 137–138
  learner experiences 131, 132–133
    data analysis 133
    data collection 131
    ethical guidelines 134
    participants' recommendations and future VE projects 134–141
  reflective writing 137–138

W

work-life balance
  COVID-19, impact of 50, 52

www.ingramcontent.com/pod-product-compliance
Lightning Source LLC
Chambersburg PA
CBHW050032090426
42735CB00022B/3457